SpringerBriefs in Child Development

D0771489

For further volumes:
http://www.springer.com/series/10210

Bradford H. Pillow

Children's Discovery of the Active Mind

Phenomenological Awareness, Social Experience, and Knowledge About Cognition

 Springer

Bradford H. Pillow
Department of Psychology
Northern Illinois University
DeKalb, IL 60115
USA
e-mail: pillow@niu.edu

ISSN 2192-838X   e-ISSN 2192-8398
ISBN 978-1-4614-2247-1   e-ISBN 978-1-4614-2248-8
DOI 10.1007/978-1-4614-2248-8
Springer New York Dordrecht Heidelberg London

Library of Congress Control Number: 2011942906

Printed on acid-free paper

Springer is part of Springer Science+Business Media (www.springer.com)

Dedicated to the memory of my parents, Jack and Betty Pillow

Acknowledgments

My interest in children's understanding of the mind began as a graduate student at Stanford University, where I was privileged to work with John Flavell. John's work has been a continuing source of insight and inspiration. I thank him for his guidance, encouragement, and support. I thank my own current graduate student, RaeAnne Pearson, for editorial assistance with this manuscript and for many thought-provoking discussions of research. I thank Elizabeth Yun for encouragement to pursue this project, and Matthew for his boundless enthusiasm for life and an endless stream of words and ideas. And I thank Judy Jones and Garth Haller at Springer for their efforts throughout the publishing process.

Contents

About the Author

Bradford Pillow, Ph.D., is Associate Professor of Psychology at Northern Illinois University. Since receiving his Ph.D. in Psychology from Stanford University in 1986, he has conducted research on the development of metacognition and social cognition in preschool children, elementary school children, and adolescents. His research focuses primarily on children's ability to infer another person's knowledge, beliefs, or visual experience, children's understanding of cognitive processes such as attention, inference, comprehension, and memory, children's ability to monitor their own cognitive states, and children's explanations of another person's behavior. Currently, he is Associate Editor for *The Journal of Genetic Psychology*, and Consulting Editor for *Child Development*.

Chapter 1
Learning About Cognitive Activities

Abstract Reasoning about cognitive activities and epistemic states is important for both social interaction and academic tasks. Developmental changes in children's understanding of cognition have been documented from early childhood through adolescence, including concepts of attention, memory, inference, and the stream of consciousness, and reasoning about the nature of knowledge and truth. The goals of this book are to trace developmental changes in those concepts and to identify experiences that inform children's concepts of cognitive activities. This chapter outlines a model integrating (a) children's conceptual knowledge of mental functioning, (b) children's phenomenological awareness of their own cognitive activities, and (c) children's social experience. According to the proposed model, the development of knowledge of cognitive activities is driven by combinations of these three types of information about mental functioning.

While driving to preschool on a snowy Wisconsin morning, I had the following conversation with my son, who was six days away from his fifth birthday:

Matthew: Naiya got a toy violin for Christmas.

Me: She did? That's nice.

Matthew: She already knew that I have two violins. I guess she must have memory.

By attributing memory to his classmate, Matthew evidenced some understanding of mental life. Implicitly, he recognized that different people know different things. Further, he seemed to appreciate that Naiya's awareness of his violins, a fact that she had been introduced to several months earlier, required some retention of previously encountered information.

The fact that five-year-olds know something about memory would not surprise many parents of young children. Nor would it surprise developmental psychologists. The past 40 years of research on metamemory indicates that by five years of age, if not earlier, children possess at least some basic knowledge about the occurrence of remembering and forgetting. But this early knowledge of memory

B. H. Pillow, *Children's Discovery of the Active Mind,*
SpringerBriefs in Child Development, DOI: 10.1007/978-1-4614-2248-8_1,
© Bradford H. Pillow 2012

raises questions about the development of children's concepts of cognitive activities. How broad is children's knowledge of cognitive activities? People may attend selectively to information in their environment, store some of it in memory, retrieve it for later recall, or draw inferences from it, whether valid or not, or people may make unfounded guesses and baseless assertions. Which cognitive activities do children of different ages know about? How deep, rich, or detailed is their understanding of any particular aspect of cognition? And how do children learn about cognitive activities?

Reasoning about cognitive activities and epistemic states figures prominently in a wide range of everyday endeavors. During social interactions assumptions about others' thoughts guide a person's own actions and frame the interpretation of others' actions. In academic settings knowledge about cognition influences students' selection of learning strategies, and cognitive monitoring aids students' evaluation of their performance. Conceptions of the nature of knowledge also contribute to the abilities to reflect on one's own thought processes and evaluate the reasoning of others, which are important for critical thinking and understanding of science. Furthermore, the emergence and elaboration of children's concepts of cognitive activities may function as a developmental bridge between young children's understanding of mental states and adolescents' and adults' epistemological thought. Therefore, to construct a comprehensive picture of epistemological development, it is important to describe developmental trends in children's concepts of cognitive activities and to identify experiences that inform developmental change.

Children's understanding of knowledge and cognition changes greatly from early childhood through adolescence. Developmental changes have been documented in many aspects of children's awareness and understanding of mental functioning, including children's recognition of individual differences in knowledge and belief, children's reports of the content of their own thoughts, children's memory for the sources of their beliefs, children's understanding of cognitive activities such as attention, memory, and inference, children's monitoring of their own memory, comprehension, and certainty, and adolescents' reasoning about the nature of knowledge and truth. Although a large research literature has examined young children's understanding of knowledge, belief, and intentions, and another body of work has investigated adolescents' and adult's epistemological thought, the development of concepts of mental functioning during middle and late childhood has received less attention. Moreover, findings concerning understanding of different aspects of cognition across the age span from early childhood to adolescence have remained largely unrelated to each other. Developmental processes that may contribute to children's understanding of the mind, such as theory change, introspection, and socio-cultural learning, often have been treated as rival alternatives, rather than interrelated aspects of social cognitive growth. Despite important differences among these approaches, they complement each other in some regards. In particular, competing accounts of social cognitive development emphasize different sources of information that may contribute to children's learning about the mind. Because understanding of mental functioning likely derives from multiple sources, at least some aspects of these different approaches may be amenable to integration.

This book presents a framework for conceptualizing developmental changes in children's awareness and understanding of cognitive activities. My purpose is to trace developmental changes in those concepts and to identify experiences that inform children's concepts of cognitive activities. Three fundamental questions about any area of conceptual development are: (a) what changes occur in children's understanding?, (b) what information do children utilize for learning?, and (c) what learning processes underlie conceptual change? My emphasis will be on the first two questions: what changes occur and what information is available as a source of learning, though I will speculate briefly about learning processes as well. Below I outline a model integrating (a) children's conceptual knowledge of mental functioning, (b) children's phenomenological awareness of their own cognitive activities, and (c) children's social experience. According to the proposed model, the development of knowledge of cognitive activities is driven by combinations of these three types of information about mental functioning, rather than depending upon a single source of information. Then in later chapters, I discuss the development of each of the three components in the model and review relevant empirical findings.

1.1 Conceptual Knowledge, Phenomenological Awareness and Social Experience

As adults, we know a great deal about mental life. We know that recognizing a familiar face is easier than recalling a name, that becoming absorbed in a phone conversation while driving may lead one to drive two miles past a freeway exit without noticing it, that a tune played on the public address system of grocery store may cue idiosyncratic associations with long ago people or places, and that advocates of contrasting political positions may construe the same events in different ways, and much more. Moreover, we understand these specific phenomena in terms of psychological processes such as memory, attention, and biased interpretation. Where do our concepts of cognition come from? How do we learn about our own minds and those of others? In this section, I provide a brief overview of the proposed model, in which I seek to explain the development of children's knowledge of cognition by integrating conceptual knowledge of cognitive activities with information available through cognitive monitoring and social experience.

On the surface, explaining how children form concepts of cognitive activities poses a problem. Much of cognitive processing is assumed to occur outside of conscious awareness. For example, Mandler (1975) argued that only the outcomes of unconscious processes are available to conscious evaluation. Not only would a lack of introspective access seem to prevent learning through first-person

Table 1.1 Components of the model

Conceptual knowledge	Phenomenological awareness	Social experience
Knowledge of mental states	Informational content	Observation
Knowledge of cognitive activities:	Informational source	Social interaction
Occurrence knowledge	Feelings of effort or difficulty	Formal education
Organizational knowledge	Feelings of certainty or clarity	
Epistemological thought	Emotion	

experience, it also would hinder social transmission of experiences from one individual to another. Without introspective access, individuals would have no direct first-person knowledge of cognition to pass on through verbal communication. Moreover, other person's cognitive processes are unobservable and are not necessarily manifested in any immediate and systematic expressive cues or action patterns. Therefore, three sources of information, introspection, verbal communication, and observation of overt behavior, might all seem to be unavailable for learning about the occurrence and nature of cognitive activities. I argue that these sources are, in fact, available to some degree. Though each source by itself is limited, in combination with each other, and in combination with children's already developing knowledge of mental states, they become informative. Similarly, Lillard (1999) proposes that young children's understanding of mental states is informed by interactions among introspection, culture, and detection of analogies between self and other. Kuhn (2000) also characterizes metacognitive knowledge as developing through the interplay of social processes and reflection on first-person experience, and Moore (2006) argues that the integration of first-person and third-person perspectives through social interaction during infancy provides the foundation for social understanding.

In the model proposed here, three general components of metacognitive development are related: (a) conceptual knowledge of cognitive activities, (b) phenomenological awareness, and (c) social experience. Conceptual knowledge is informed by phenomenological awareness and social experience, and there is also reciprocal influence among these three components. This chapter provides a brief overview of the model. Each of the three components is described below (see Table 1.1 for a summary), and patterns of influence among them are outlined. In later sections, empirical evidence is presented concerning developmental changes and relations among conceptual knowledge of cognition, phenomenological awareness, and social experience.

1.1.1 Conceptual Knowledge About Cognitive Activities and Mental States

Conceptual knowledge refers to relatively stable knowledge of mental states and cognitive activities that can be used to assess another person's mental state, predict one's own future mental state, construct an explanation for one's current mental state, or reconstruct past mental states (e.g. Flavell 1981; Kuhn 2000; Wellman 1990). Knowledge of cognitive activities can be distinguished from knowledge about mental states (Pillow 1995). For present purposes, knowledge about mental states refers to knowledge about potentially expressible epistemic, affective, or intentional content (i.e., knowledge, ignorance, beliefs, emotions, desires, motives, intentions, etc.), with the emphasis here being on knowledge about epistemic states. Knowledge about cognitive activities refers to knowledge concerning processes that generate, select, manipulate, transform, or operate on mental states, including both automatic and deliberate processes (i.e., attending, remembering, forgetting, inferring, guessing, using problem solving strategies or memory strategies, etc.). In the empirical literature, research on three aspects of conceptual understanding of cognitive activities can be distinguished: (a) occurrence knowledge, (b) organizational knowledge, and (c) epistemological thought. Occurrence knowledge means understanding that cognitive activities occur, including recognition of the typical outcomes of a cognitive activity and recognition of situations in which an activity is likely to occur. Organizational knowledge refers to beliefs about functional relations, similarities, and differences among cognitive activities (e.g. Schwanenflugel et al. 1994).

Epistemological thought includes general assumptions about the nature of knowledge and the relation between the mind and reality (e.g. Chandler 1987; King and Kitchener 1994; Kuhn 2001; Hofer and Pintrich 2002; Moshman 2005).

1.1.2 Sources of Information About Cognitive Activities

In the proposed model, phenomenological awareness and social experience inform children's conceptual understanding of cognition. Phenomenological awareness of cognitive activities refers to conscious experiences associated with cognitive processing (c.f. Flavell 1981; Humphrey 1983; Johnson 1988; Lillard 1999; Mandler 1975). Awareness of five aspects of cognition is distinguished here: (a) informational content, (b) informational source, (c) feelings of effort or difficulty, (d) feelings of certainty or uncertainty, clarity or confusion, and (e) emotional experiences associated with, or arising from, cognitive activities or their outcomes. These five aspects of phenomenological awareness are potentially informative about the occurrence and characteristics of cognitive activities. Moreover, these sorts of awareness are featured in prominent theories of consciousness or metacognition (e.g. Flavell 1981; Johnson et al. 1993; Mandler 1975; Nelson and Narens 1990). Thus, there is reason to believe they are available, at least to adults, and could inform learning about the mind. Social experience can be a source of metacognitive knowledge, as insights into cognitive functioning emerge during social interactions or are transmitted in social contexts (c.f. Harris et al. 2005; Moore 2006; Tomasello 1999b). Such insights may occur during (a) observation of other persons' actions, (b) participation in social interactions, and (c) engagement in cultural activities and institutions. Through social experience individuals may learn about their own cognitive functioning or the cognitive functioning of others.

1.1.3 Patterns of Influence

Children's conceptual knowledge of mental states provides a foundation for learning about cognitive activities. Noticing changes in mental states could facilitate learning about the occurrence of cognitive activities. Thus, by providing cues to changes in mental states, phenomenological awareness and social experience, in combination with children's early concepts of mental states may lead to the emergence of an initial understanding of the occurrence of cognitive activities. Through further experience, this initial understanding could be elaborated, eventually giving rise to organizational knowledge and epistemological thought.

Conceptual knowledge, phenomenological awareness, and social experience are not independent; they permeate each other. Four general patterns of influence are identified in the proposed model: (a) reciprocal influence between phenomenological awareness and conceptual knowledge, (b) reciprocal influence between phenomenological awareness and social experience, (c) reciprocal influence between social experience and conceptual knowledge, and (d) pathways involving all three components of the model (see Fig. 1.1). These possible patterns of influence are outlined below.

Reciprocal influence between phenomenological awareness and conceptual knowledge of cognitive activities is a feature of theories of metacognition (Flavell 1981; Koriat 1998; Lories and Schelstraete 1998) and consciousness (Humphrey 1983, 1986; Mandler 2002). Children's monitoring of metacognitive cues concerning informational content, informational source, level of certainty, and level of effort, as well as children's monitoring of emotion, provides evidence about the occurrence of cognitive processing and the characteristics of particular cognitive activities. At the same time, children's beliefs about mental functioning influence how they interpret metacognitive cues. In the present model, each of the three aspects of conceptual understanding (occurrence knowledge, organizational knowledge, and epistemological thought) participates in reciprocal influence with monitoring and interpretation of conscious cues.

Social experience and phenomenological awareness of cognitive activities also influence each other bidirectionally. On the one hand, social experience can stimulate and guide children's monitoring and interpretation of metacognitive experiences. On the other hand, children's monitoring of their own cognition can enhance their understanding of their social partners' actions and messages. These effects may occur during processes of observation, social interaction, or participation in cultural activities (e.g. Hughes and Dunn 1997; McGivern et al. 1990; Rogoff 1990; Tomasello 1999b).

In addition, social experience influences conceptual understanding of cognitive activities. Information about cognitive functioning can be socially transmitted (e.g. Moore 2006; Rogoff 1990; Tomasello 1999b). For example, adults may comment on their own thinking, children's thinking, or the thought processes of a third party (e.g. Dunn 1999; Peterson and Slaughter 2003; Ruffman et al. 2002; Sabbagh and Callanan 1998). Children's conceptual understanding of cognitive activities can

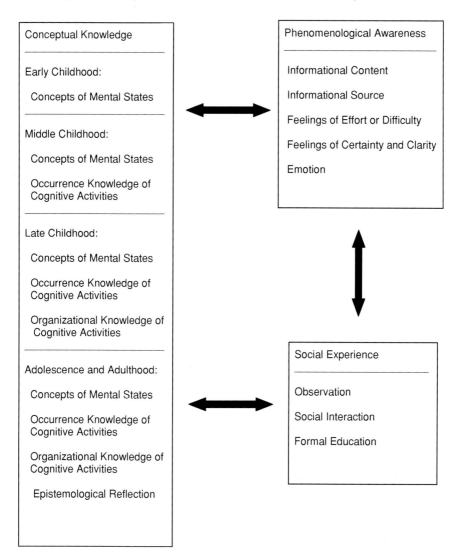

Fig. 1.1 Relations among conceptual knowledge, phenomenological awareness, and social experience

also influence children's understanding of others. Children's existing beliefs about cognition may influence what aspects of another person's behavior children notice, or how children construe another person's actions or verbal messages.

Because phenomenological awareness, social experience, and conceptual understanding of cognitive activities participate in a network of influences, complex patterns of effects also are possible. Pathways can be traced starting from any of the three components of the model, with either of the other two components mediating influence on the third component. Thus, six such pathways are possible. In one pathway social experience contributes directly to children's conceptual knowledge of cognitive activities, which in turn influences phenomenological awareness. In another pathway, by directly affecting cognitive monitoring, social experience can indirectly influence the development of conceptual knowledge. Likewise, the influence of phenomenological awareness on conceptual knowledge may be mediated by social factors, or the influence of phenomenological aware-ness on social experience may be mediated by children's conceptual understanding of cognition. Conceptual knowledge may also have indirect effects on either phenomenological awareness or social experience.

Phenomenological awareness and social experience may jointly inform children's understanding of cognitive activities. As they learn about cognition, children may rely on general learning processes to integrate their mental state concepts with information available through first-person phenomenological experience and social experience. That is, both general pattern recognition abilities and executive function may enable children to develop concepts of cognitive activities from the available inputs.

1.2 Summary

Distinguishing specific aspects of conceptual knowledge about cognitive activities, phenomenological awareness, and social experience, and identifying possible patterns of influence among them is useful for organizing the empirical literature and suggesting directions for future research. The next three chapters review research on the development of conceptual knowledge of cognitive activities, phenomenological awareness of cognitive processing, and social influences on metacognitive understanding, respectively.

In Chap. 2, I address the question of what changes occur in children's under-standing of mental functioning. Age-related changes in children's knowledge of particular cognitive activities are described. Using the distinctions among occur-rence knowledge, organizational knowledge, and epistemological thought as an organizational framework, I review research concerning children's understanding of the stream of consciousness, attention, memory, inference, imagination, rela-tions between thoughts and emotions, and the controllability of thought. Then research on children's knowledge of similarities and differences among cognitive processes is discussed, followed by consideration of epistemological development in adolescence and adulthood.

In Chaps. 3 and 4, I address the sources of information that children use to learn about cognitive activities. For my proposal concerning patterns of learning to have a chance at being correct, at the very least children would have to (a) have some ability to monitor their own cognitive states or activities, and (b) participate in social experiences that provide information about cognitive functioning. In addi-tion, age-related changes in cognitive monitoring or social experience could have implications for conceptual development. In Chap. 3, I discuss the development of cognitive monitoring, and consider monitoring as a potential source of information about cognitive activities. Theories of consciousness (i.e. Humphrey 1983, 1986; Koriat 1998; Mandler 2002) and metacognition (i.e. Flavell 1981; Johnson et al. 1993; Kuhn 2000) frame the discussion. Then, I focus on studies concerning monitoring of informational content, informational source, feelings of effort, feelings of certainty, or emotion. In Chap. 4, I consider social experiences that are potentially informative about cognitive functioning. The implications of socio-cultural and social cognitive theories are discussed (i.e. Lillard 1999; Rogoff 1990; Tomasello 1999a, 1999b), and then research is presented. However, there have been few studies relevant to social influences on children's understanding of cognitive activities. Instead, most studies have examined social influences on mental state understanding, especially influences on young children's under-standing of belief and emotion. This literature is summarized briefly and the possibility of cultural differences in the development of children's understanding of cognitive activities is discussed.

Following the discussion of these three main components, I then seek to inte-grate conceptual knowledge, phenomenological awareness, and social experience by elaborating on possible patterns of influence among them in Chap. 5. Although this section is speculative, relevant empirical evidence is discussed where avail-able. In addition, I consider possible developmental mechanisms underlying the acquisition of knowledge about cognitive activities, focusing on the issue of domain-specific modules versus domain-general learning processes Finally, in Chap. 6, I conclude by first discussing insights from three general approaches to conceptualizing children's knowledge about the mind: (a) a theory metaphor, (b) a perceptual metaphor, and (c) socio-cultural theories, and then suggesting direc-tions for future research.

References

Chandler, M. J. (1987). The othello effect: Essay on the emergence and eclipse of skeptical doubt. *Human Development, 30,* 137–159.

Dunn, J. (1999). Making sense of the social world: Mindreading, emotion, and relationships. In P. D. Zelazo, J. W. Astington, & D. R. Olson (Eds.), *Developing theories of intention:Social understanding and self-control* (pp. 229–242). Mahwah: Erlbaum.

Flavell, J. H. (1981). Cognitive monitoring. In W. P. Dickson (Ed.), *Children's oral communication skills* (pp. 35–60). New York: Academic.

Harris, P. L., de Rosnay, M., & Pons, F. (2005). Language and children's understanding of mental states. *Current Directions in Psychological Science, 14,* 69–73.

Hofer, B. K., & Pintrich, P. R. (2002). *Personal epistemology: The psychology of beliefs about knowledge and knowing.* Mahwah: Lawrence Erlbaum Associates.

Hughes, C., & Dunn, J. (1997). Pretend you didn't know: Preschoolers' talk about mental states in pretend play. *Cognitive Development, 12,* 477–499.

Humphrey, N. (1983). *Consciousness regained: Chapters in the development of mind Oxford.* Oxford: Oxford University Press.

Humphrey, N. (1986). *The inner eye*. London: Faber and Faber.

Johnson, C. N. (1988). Theory of mind and the structure of conscious experience. In J. W. Astington, P. L. Harris, & D. R. Olson (Eds.), *Developing theories of mind* (pp. 47–63). New York: Cambridge University Press.

Johnson, M. K., Hashtroudi, S., & Lindsay, D. S. (1993). Source monitoring. *Psychological Bulletin, 114*, 3–28.

King, P. M., & Kitchener, K. (1994). *Developing reflective judgment: Understanding and promoting intellectual growth and critical thinking in adolescents and adults*. San Francisco: Jossey-Bass.

Koriat, A. (1998). Illusions of knowing: The link between knowledge and metaknowledge. In V. Y. Yzerbyt, G. Lories, & B. Dardenne (Eds.), *Metacognition: Cognitive and social dimensions* (pp. 16–34). London: Sage Publications.

Kuhn, D. (2000). Theory of mind, metacognition, and reasoning: A life-span perspective. In P. Mitchell & K. J. Riggs (Eds.), *Children's reasoning and the mind* (pp. 301–326). Hove: Psychology Press.

Kuhn, D. (2001). How do people know? *Psychological Science, 12*, 1–8.

Lillard, A. (1999). Developing a cultural theory of mind: The CIAO approach. *CurrentDirections in Psychological Science, 8*, 57–61.

Lories, G., & Schelstraete, M. (1998). The feeling-of-knowing as a judgment. In V. Y. Yzerbyt, G. Lories, & B. Dardenne (Eds.), *Metacognition: Cognitive and social dimensions* (pp. 53–68). London: Sage Publications.

Mandler, G. (1975). Consciousness: Respectable, useful, and probably necessary. In R. Solso (Ed.), *Information processing and cognition: The loyola symposium* (pp. 229–254). Hillsdale: Lawrence Erlbaum Associates.

Mandler, G. (2002). *Consciousness recovered: Psychological functions and origins of conscious thought*. Amsterdam: John Benjamins Publishing Company.

McGivern, J. E., Levin, J. R., Pressley, M., & Ghatala, E. S. (1990). A developmental study of memory monitoring and strategy selection. *Contemporary Educational Psychology, 15*, 103–115.

Moore, C. (2006). *The development of commonsense psychology*. Mahwah: Lawrence Erlbaum Associates.

Moshman, D. (2005). *Adolescent psychological development: Rationality, morality, and identity* (2nd ed.). Mahwah: Lawrence Erlbaum Associates.

Nelson, T. O., & Narens, L. (1990). Metamemory: A theoretical framework and some new findings. In G. Bower (Ed.), *The psychology of learning and motivation* (pp. 125–173). San Diego: Academic.

Peterson, C., & Slaughter, V. (2003). Opening windows into the mind: Mothers' preferences for mental state explanations and children's theory of mind. *Cognitive Development, 18*, 399–429.

Pillow, B. H. (1995). Two trends in the development of conceptual perspective-taking: An elaboration of the passive-active hypothesis. *International Journal of Behavioral Development, 18*, 649–676.

Rogoff, B. (1990). *Apprenticeship in thinking: Cognitive development in social context*. New York: Oxford University Press.

Ruffman, T., Slade, L., & Crowe, E. (2002). The relation between children's and mothers' mental state language and theory-of-mind understanding. *Child Development, 73*, 734–751.

Sabbagh, M. A., & Callanan, M. A. (1998). Metarepresentation in action: 3-, 4-, and 5-year-olds' developing theories of mind in parent-child conversations. *Developmental Psychology, 34*, 491–502.

Schwanenflugel, P. J., Fabricius, W. V., & Alexander, J. (1994). Developing theories of mind: Understanding concepts and relations between mental activities. *Child Development, 65*, 1546–1563.

Tomasello, M. (1999a). Having intentions, understanding intentions, and understanding communicative intentions. In P. D. Zelazo, J. W. Astington, & D. R. Olson (Eds.),

Developing theories of intention: Social understanding and self-control (pp. 63–76). Mahwah: Lawrence Erlbaum Associates.

Tomasello, M. (1999b). *The cultural origins of human cognition.* Cambridge: Harvard University Press.

Wellman, H. M. (1990). *The child's theory of mind.* Cambridge: MIT Press.

Chapter 2
Conceptual Knowledge About Cognitive Activities

Abstract Empirical research concerning developmental changes in children's understanding of cognitive activities is reviewed. Age-related changes in children's knowledge of seven aspects of cognitive functioning are considered: (a) the stream of consciousness, (b) attention, (c) memory, (d) inference, (e) imagination, (f) relations between thoughts and emotions, and (g) the controllability of thoughts. Three general levels of understanding are distinguished: (a) occurrence knowledge: knowledge of the occurrence of particular cognitive activity, (b) organizational knowledge: knowledge of similarities and differences in the functions of cognitive activities, and (c) epistemological thought: broad, abstract thinking about the nature of knowledge and mind.

When my son was five and half years old, we had the following conversation in the kitchen:

Matthew: *Can I have some juice?*
Me: *Sure. What kind? Apple or orange?*
Matthew: *I don't know.*
Me: *Then I'll give you apple.*
Matthew: *That's not the one I want.*
Me: *What do you want?*
Matthew: *You know…*
Me: *Which one?*
Matthew: *You know which one because I told you it's not apple.*

Clearly, Matthew understood the logic of deduction by elimination, and despite not being particularly helpful in his choice of communicative strategies, he was generous enough to credit me with the ability to infer his juice preference. Thus, his knowledge of reasoning allowed him to infer my knowledge. Two days later, while driving to a Fourth of July fireworks display, he explained, "In my imagination I can see the fireworks. A brown sky with exploding colors." In addition to his previous recognition that people may actively reason about the world, drawing

B. H. Pillow, *Children's Discovery of the Active Mind,*
SpringerBriefs in Child Development, DOI: 10.1007/978-1-4614-2248-8_2,
© Bradford H. Pillow 2012

conclusions by combining premises, here Matthew also revealed knowledge about another sort of cognitive activity. Commenting on his own internal fireworks display indicated awareness that the mind can generate thoughts and images extending beyond the immediate situation. My goal in this chapter is largely descriptive. I review empirical research on children's understanding of mental states and cognitive activities, using the distinctions among occurrence knowledge, organizational knowledge, and epistemological thought to frame the literature.

Knowledge about the mind is evident in early childhood, as 2 and 3-year-olds talk and reason about both their own mental states and those of others. In everyday conversation 2 and 3-year-olds frequently refer to mental states, including emotions and desires, and 4-year-olds increasing talk about knowledge, thoughts, and beliefs (Bartsch and Wellman 1995; Dunn 1999; Wellman et al. 1995), and even preverbal infants display sensitivity to others intentions, knowledge, and beliefs (Onishi and Baillargeon 2005; Woodward 2009). In experimental studies, 2 and 3-year-olds demonstrate awareness of another person's visual perspective and recognition of others' knowledge or ignorance (e.g., Flavell et al. 1978; Moll and Tomasello 2006; Pillow 1989a; Pratt and Bryant 1990). Although 3-year-olds typically have difficulty in understanding false beliefs, by 4–5 years of age children appreciate that a person's beliefs may contrast with reality (e.g., Hogrefe et al. 1986). Young children also distinguish among basic emotions, such as happiness, sadness, anger, and fear, and relate specific emotions to different kinds of situations (Harris 1989). In addition, young children appear to have some understanding of intentions. By 3 years of age, children distinguish between intended outcomes and unintended outcomes (Shultz and Wells 1985), and by 5 years of age children appear to understand that intentions play a causal role in producing action (Astington 1993). Thus, by three years of age, children have begun to recognize knowledge, ignorance, desire, and emotion, and around 4–5 years of age children begin to understand belief (see Flavell and Miller 1998 for a review). Children's early understanding of mental states, such as desire, intention, knowledge and beliefs, is impressive, especially in view of the once prevalent assumption that young children do not clearly differentiate between mental states and physical events and are unable to conceive of another person's perspective as different from their own (e.g., Broughton 1978; Piaget 1929; Selman 1980).

Despite their impressive understanding of mental states, young children's social understanding is far from mature. Wellman (1990) proposed that young children and adults share the same basic conceptual framework for reasoning about human action. According to Wellman, both children and adults understand human action within a framework of belief-desire reasoning. Within this framework, actions are seen to result from desires and beliefs, desires often are seen to be derived from physiological states or emotions, and beliefs often are seen to result from perceptual experiences. Therefore, observed actions are explained in terms of a person's beliefs and desires, and information about beliefs and desires is used to predict future actions. This view is supported by evidence that 3 and 4-year-olds often explain and predict actions in terms of desires and beliefs (Bartsch and

Wellman 1989). Thus, concepts of mental states are central to children's understanding of human behavior from an early age. Although the same basic mentalistic framework for social understanding persists from early childhood through adulthood, Wellman further proposed that a more elaborated understanding of mental functioning and human action emerges later in childhood. This more elaborated framework includes both a greater variety of concepts and new links among core concepts. For example, in addition to realizing that beliefs derive from perceptual experience, adults and older children also realize that cognitive activities, such as reasoning, remembering, and forgetting, can influence beliefs. This proposed shift from a simple belief-desire framework to a more elaborated framework implies that during middle and late childhood, children's should develop greater understanding of cognitive processes that generate, select, manipulate, transform, or operate on mental states (i.e., attending, remembering, forgetting, inferring, guessing, using problem solving strategies or memory strategies, etc.) and concepts of cognitive processes should become increasingly central to children's understanding of psychological functioning and behavior.

Several theorists have suggested a more specific transition in children's understanding of cognitive activities occurs at approximately 6 or 7 years of age (Chandler 1988; Chandler and Boyes 1982; Higgins 1981; Pillow 1988, 1995; Taylor 1988). Chandler (1988) (Chandler and Boyes 1982; Carpendale and Chandler 1996) proposed that prior to age 6 or 7 years children regard knowledge as an objective copy of external reality and do not grasp the possibility of multiple, subjective interpretations of the same input, and Taylor (1988) suggested that young children equate seeing with knowing. Higgins (1981) made a similar distinction between differences in situational viewpoints, which are due to persons being in different circumstances, and individual viewpoints, which are due to persons having different individual characteristics such as personality traits, attitudes, or beliefs. According to Higgins (1981) differences in situational viewpoints may be easier to understand. These theories imply that (a) young children should understand a direct connection between perceptual experience and knowledge, (b) young children may not recognize how cognitive activities mediate between perceived information and a person's representation of the world, and (c) beginning around 6 or 7 years of age children should begin to understand that individuals differing in their prior experience or expectations may interpret the same information differently. More generally, children age years or older may begin to recognize the occurrence and effects of processes such as memory, attention, and inference (Pillow 1995).

The prediction that young children recognize the perceptual origins of mental states is supported by studies of early perspective-taking. As early as 2 years of age, children's non-verbal behavior demonstrates awareness of another person's visual perspective (e.g., Flavell et al. 1978; Moll and Tomasello 2006). Three-year-olds can report what object another person sees, and 4 and 5-year-olds can report how an object looks to another person (e.g., Masangkay et al. 1974). Three and four-year-olds also recognize that another person's knowledge or ignorance about a hidden toy depends upon the person has seen the toy or not (Pillow 1989a; Pratt and Bryant 1990).

Despite this early understanding of perceptual influences on knowledge, young children often do not seem to appreciate those activities such as selective attention, inference, or interpretation also may influence knowledge and belief (Pillow 1995). Knowledge of cognitive activities begins to appear between 5 and 7 years of age. For example, 5 and 6-year-olds recognize that people attend selectively (e.g., Flavell et al. 1995; Pillow 1989b), interpret information constructively (e.g., Carpendale and Chandler 1996; Pillow and Henrichon 1996), and make deductive inferences (e.g., Sodian and Wimmer 1987). However, young children do appear to understand some instances of cognitive activity. In particular, 3 and 4-year-olds recognize that encountering a situation associated with past emotional experiences can cue present thoughts and feelings (Lagattuta and Wellman 2001). This research is reviewed below.

2.1 Levels of Understanding

Three aspects of conceptual understanding of cognitive activities can be distinguished: (a) occurrence knowledge, (b) organizational knowledge, and (c) epistemological thought. These three aspects of children's conceptual knowledge of cognitive activities are not a sequence of distinct developmental stages. Because each has a gradual, protracted development, they may overlap each other, and influence each other, to some degree. Nevertheless, a general developmental progression can be traced in the research literature. Much of children's occurrence knowledge first appears during the transition from early to middle childhood (roughly 5–7 years of age) and increases thereafter. Knowledge of mental functioning is organized during early childhood; however, an adult-like organization of knowledge about mental activities begins to emerge during late childhood (roughly 9–10 years of age) and is further refined between late childhood and early adulthood. Some forms of epistemological thought are evident during early adolescence (roughly 13–14 years of age), but epistemological thought continues to develop through adulthood, and there are substantial individual differences among adults' intuitive epistemologies. Distinguishing occurrence knowledge, organizational knowledge, and epistemological thought provides a useful framework for organizing the empirical literature on children's concepts of cognition and examining developmental trends. Below, I describe empirical evidence concerning developmental changes in knowledge of the occurrence of cognitive activities, in the organization of children's concepts of cognition, and in epistemological thought. I also consider developmental relations among these three levels of understanding.

2.1.1 Occurrence Knowledge

Occurrence knowledge refers to understanding that cognitive activities occur, including recognition of the typical outcomes of a cognitive activity and recognition of situations in which an activity is likely to occur. Occurrence knowledge includes both knowledge of automatic activities and knowledge of the availability and effects of deliberate strategic activities. Adults typically know about a variety of cognitive activities, but their knowledge may be limited. Even adults may not possess explicit models of specific information-processing mechanisms. Instead, conceptions of cognitive activities often may consist of (a) knowledge of the outcomes of cognitive activities, (b) knowledge of the antecedent conditions, both internal and external, that precede those outcomes, (c) some notion of mental activity linking antecedents and outcomes, and (d) knowledge of some properties of cognitive activities. For instance, rather than having a detailed model of a selective attention mechanism, people generally may know that a person watching television in a crowded room, with several conversations going on nearby, may comprehend and remember information from the television program, but not know what was said in the surrounding conversations. This outcome may be attributed to a process of paying attention or blocking out extraneous information, and this process may be regarded as limited in capacity, effortful, and subject to distraction, depending upon an individual's particular knowledge and beliefs about attention.

Children's understanding of seven aspects of cognitive functioning is considered below: (a) the stream of consciousness, (b) attention, (c) memory, (d) inference, (e) imagination, (f) relations between thoughts and emotions, and (g) the controllability of thoughts. Knowing about the stream of consciousness, attention, memory, and inference is central to understanding the mind as an active processor of information. Knowledge of the stream of consciousness suggests recognition of continual cognitive activity as a fundamental part of mental life, and knowledge of attention, memory, and inference is central for understanding how people process and represent information about the environment. Knowledge of imagination would indicate awareness of processes that internally generated and not necessarily aimed at representing external reality. Recognizing that cognition and emotion influence each other is important for understanding that cognitive processes do not occur in isolation but are part of a larger system. Because cognition involves both controlled and automatic processes, learning about the limits of deliberate control is central for understanding the nature of mental life. Of course, children and adults also may learn about other aspects of cognition, such as planning, decision-making, mathematical calculation, reading, and even cognitive monitoring. However, there are research literatures on the seven aspects of cognition covered here, and this research provides a picture of children's developing understanding of cognitive activity.

2.1.1.1 Knowledge of the Stream of Consciousness

Knowledge of the stream of consciousness could include recognition that there is ongoing, continual mental activity and recognition that one thought can cue associated thoughts. Flavell and his colleagues have investigated children's understanding of both of these aspects of consciousness. Young children often do not seem aware that thoughts continue to occur in the absence of over activity. Compared to children ages 5–7 years, 4-year-olds are less likely to attribute thoughts to a person who is waiting quietly, listening, looking, or reading (Flavell et al. 1993, 1995). For example, most 4-year-olds judge that the mind of person who is waiting quietly is "empty of thoughts and ideas" or "not doing anything", unlike 6–7-year-olds and adults who credit the waiting person with having "some thoughts and ideas." (Flavell et al. 1993). In fact, 4-year-olds often under-attribute thought even to a person who is described as looking, listening, or reading (Flavell et al. 1995). In addition, 4-year-olds often deny the possibility of covert inner speech (Flavell et al. 1997), but most 4-year-olds do attribute thought to a person silently puzzling over a problem (Flavell et al. 1993). Thus, although 4-year-olds have some understanding that conscious thought may occur even in the absence of overt activity, they do not regard the stream of consciousness as continuous, nor do they associate conscious thought with inner speech. By 5–8 years of age children begin to show greater knowledge of conscious mental activity.

Young children demonstrate some limited understanding of cognitive cuing. In a simple hiding task, 3-year-olds often recognize placing a closely associated cue at the location where a target item is hidden (e.g., placing a picture of a hose over a folder containing a picture of a firefighter), may help another person find the hidden object; however, 3-year-olds typically fail to recognize the utility of more remote or arbitrary cues (e.g., placing a picture of sailboat over a folder containing a picture of mailman who enjoys sailing) (Gordon and Flavell 1977). Furthermore, prior to 8 or 9 years of age children have difficulty in evaluating the informativeness of a cue (Beal 1985), and prior to 6 years of age children often fail to distinguish between strongly associated and weakly associated cues when choosing a cue to either facilitate or hinder another person's search for a hidden object (Sodian and Schneider 1990). Understanding of emotional may begin relatively early. Thus, 3 and 4-year-olds show some appreciation that being reminded of past emotional experiences can cue associated thoughts that affect a person's current emotional state (Lagattuta and Wellman 2001).

Overall, studies of children's understanding of the occurrence of ongoing thought and cognitive cuing indicated that 3 and 4-year-olds have only limited knowledge of the stream of consciousness, but 5–8-year-olds are becoming increasingly aware of the ongoing flow of mental activity.

2.1.1.2 Knowledge of Attention

Developing a concept of attention is an important part of understanding the subjectivity of knowledge. Because our attentional capacity is limited and we attend selectively, at any moment we process only a portion of the information available around us. Therefore, recognition of attentional filtering implies understanding that cognitive processes mediate between the external world and our knowledge of that world.

Children begin to understand attention as limited in capacity and selective between approximately 5 and 8 years of age. Most 4-year-olds, unlike older children, do not appreciate that a person who is focusing attentively on one message or thought probably would not fully process other information or experience additional unrelated thoughts at the same instant (Flavell et al. 1993, 1995; Miller and Bigi 1979; Pillow 1989b). For example, 7-year-olds judge that noise, such as a radio, might interfere with their ability to hear their mother calling, but only children 8-years or older recognize that reading an interesting book might result in not hearing their mother (Miller and Bigi 1979). Similarly, when asked to predict their own performance, 4-year-olds typically do not realize that focusing attention on one message or task might hinder comprehension of an incidental message (Pillow 1989b). Six and 8-year-olds judge that they would not understand an incidental message while focusing on a target task.

Furthermore, many 4-year-olds also do not understand that while concentrating on a cognitive task, a person probably would not be thinking about another irrelevant topic (Flavell et al. 1995), or that during a very brief instant a person would likely be thinking of only one thing rather than several (Flavell et al. 1993). By 5–6 years of age children begin to understand that thought may be focused on a single topic at a particular moment. In addition, many 5-year-olds also refer to a person's focus of attention to explain the person's failure to act in accordance with information available from an unattended source (Pillow and Lovett 1998). When deciding who a request for information should be addressed to, most 5-year-olds select a person whose attention is not already engaged, whereas 4-year-olds do not discriminate between a person who is listening to a radio and an adjacent person who is not listening to the radio (Pillow 1989b).

Studies of children's understanding of attention indicate that most 3- and 4-year-olds do not appreciate that attention is limited and selective. Some knowledge of attention begins to appear around 5-years of age, and understanding of attention increases during the elementary school years.

2.1.1.3 Knowledge About Memory

Knowledge of memory develops gradually from early childhood to adulthood. Although young children demonstrate some knowledge of the processes of remembering and forgetting, they know little about the effectiveness of deliberate memory strategies, such as rehearsal or categorization. During the elementary school years children increasingly differentiate among effective and ineffective strategies.

Preschool children have at least some partial understanding of remembering and forgetting. Four-year-olds, but not 3-year-olds, recognize that remembering and forgetting require prior knowledge of the remembered or forgotten information (Lyon and Flavell 1994). Five-year-olds invoke forgetting to explain mistaken actions (Pillow and Lovett 1998). However, young children's understanding of the terms "remember" and "forget" is fragile; they sometimes use these terms to refer to correct versus incorrect action, regardless of a person's prior knowledge (Wellman and Johnson 1979). Young children also have limited knowledge of factors that influence memory performance. Four-year-olds recognize that increasing the number of items on a list makes recall more difficult (Wellman 1977) and that longer retention intervals increase the likelihood of forgetting (Lyon and Flavell 1993). As mentioned previously, 3 and 4-year-olds also demonstrate some awareness that reminders of past emotional experiences can cue thoughts that influence a person's current emotion, but children's understanding of emotional cuing increases between 3 and 7 years of age (Lagattuta and Wellman 2001). With emotionally neutral materials, children under five years usually do not fully appreciate how associated cues can trigger retrieval (Gordon and Flavell 1977; Sodian and Schneider 1990). In addition, before 9 or 10 years of age, children do not know that a list of taxonomically related items is easier to recall than a list of unrelated words (Moynahan 1978). These results suggest that young children have some awareness of memory activities, but their knowledge of memory continues to increase well into the elementary school years.

Moreover, young children know little about the effectiveness of deliberate memory strategies. When asked to compare the effectiveness of strategies for free recall, 4-year-olds judged looking at the items to be recalled as more effective than naming, rehearsing, or categorizing them, and kindergartners showed no preference among these four strategies, but second- grade children judged rehearsal and categorization as more effective than naming or looking (Justice 1986). Fourth-grade children also judge categorization and rehearsal as equally effective memory strategies, whereas sixth-grade children regard categorization as more effective (Justice 1985). In addition, when selecting a strategy to aid either memorization or comprehension of verbal instructions, first-grade children often did not distinguish between a strategy that was effective for only memorization and a strategy that was effective only for comprehension, but third-grade children consistently selected the appropriate strategy for each goal (Lovett and Pillow 1995). Thus, knowledge of remembering and forgetting begins in early childhood, but develops greatly during the elementary school years.

2.1.1.4 Knowledge About Inference and Reasoning

Awareness of inferential activities is important for the development of logical reasoning, understanding science, critical thinking, and social competence. Understanding the nature of inference and logic has been argued to contribute to the development of logical reasoning during both childhood and adulthood (Moshman 1990). Scientific thinking involves awareness of theories, evidence, and the process of drawing conclusions from evidence (Carey and Smith 1993; Kuhn and Pearsall 2000). To critically analyze competing arguments or opinions, one must evaluate the reasoning and evidence on which each view is based (King and Kitchener 1994). In addition, recognizing another person's inferences can help children to assess another person's knowledge and beliefs. Such assessments help children to understand others' actions and also help to guide children's behavior during social interactions. Below I will consider research on: (a) children's understanding of inferences as a source of knowledge, (b) children's differentiation of inference from other patterns of thought and children's differentiation among different patterns of inference, and (c) children's evaluation of evidence.

Young children appear to know little about the occurrence of inferential activities, the contribution of inference to knowledge, or the difference between reasoning and other thought processes. Before 6- years of age, children often do not recognize that knowledge can be acquired through deductive inference (Keenan et al. 1994; Pillow 1999; Sodian and Wimmer 1987; Varouxaki et al. 1999). For example, after observing another person receive information that would enable the person to deduce the color of a hidden object, 4 and 5-year-olds often denied that the person knew the object's color, whereas 6-year-olds understood that another person could infer the hidden object's color without directly observing it (Sodian and Wimmer 1987). Although reducing memory demands improved 4-year-olds performance on a similar inference attribution task, 4-year-olds nevertheless often failed to attribute inferential knowledge to another observer (Keenan et al. 1994). Ruffman (1996) reported that 5-year-olds recognized that another observer might reach a false belief through inference, but often did not recognize that another observer might arrive at a true belief by inference. Thus, understanding of deductive inference as a source of knowledge does not appear to be demonstrated consistently until about 6-years of age.

Understanding of inference as a source of belief also could be demonstrated by recognition that individuals may arrive at different interpretations of ambiguous or incomplete information. The age at which children begin to understand interpretive inferences has been a topic of debate. According to Perner (1991), around 4 years of age children develop a concept of beliefs as representations of external circumstances. Furthermore, Perner (1991) argues that understanding the possibility of individual differences in representation implies understanding of the possibility of interpretive differences. Thus, Perner (1991) hypothesized that acquiring a representational understanding of belief at age 4 enables children to comprehend the possibility of false belief, to discover that beliefs are acquired through perceptual experience, and to understand beliefs as products of active interpretation. In contrast to Perner's position, several theorists have suggested that understanding of interpretation does not begin until approximately 6 or 7 years of age (Chandler 1988; Higgins 1981; Pillow 1995; Taylor 1988). Chandler (1988; Carpendale and Chandler 1996) distinguishes between understanding beliefs as products of direct perceptual experience and understanding beliefs as products of an active, constructive process that involves interpreting new experiences in light of prior beliefs. According to Chandler (1988; Carpendale and Chandler 1996), 4 and 5-year-old children understand the direct perceptual origins of belief, but only beginning around age 7 years do children begin to the interpretive origins of beliefs.

Several studies indicate that young children typically do not recognize that beliefs can be acquired through interpretive inferences (Carpendale and Chandler

1996; Chandler and Helm 1984; Taylor 1988; Taylor et al. 1991). For example, Chandler and Helm (1984) showed 4, 7, and 11-year-old children line drawings, covered the drawings so that only a small portion was visible, and then asked children to describe how this restricted portion of the drawing would be interpreted by another child who had not seen the entire drawing. Four-year-olds consistently attributed their own knowledge of the complete picture to the naive viewer who saw only the restricted view, but 7 and 11-year-olds recognized that the naive viewer would not be able to identify the subject of the drawing. Taylor (1988) also found that children under age 7 or 8 years often failed to appreciate that a naive observer would not be able to identify a drawing by seeing a small uninformative region. Carpendale and Chandler (1996) reported that although 8-year-olds recognized that ambiguous stimuli could be interpreted in more than one way, 5 and 6-year-olds did not (Carpendale and Chandler 1996). In addition, preschool children often do not realize that a listener may not understand the intended meaning of an ambiguous verbal message (Beal and Flavell 1983; Roberts and Patterson 1983; Sodian 1988).

Likewise, around 7 years of age children begin to recognize that prior experience can bias a person's interpretation of incomplete or ambiguous information (Pillow 1991; Pillow and Henrichon 1996; Pillow and Mash 1999). For instance, Pillow (1991) investigated children's understanding that prior expectations may bias the interpretation of social events. Children aged 4–8 years were told stories in which one character, the actor, performed an action that could be interpreted in either of two ways (e.g., as taking something out of or putting it into a container). Two other characters, the observers, held contrasting biases concerning the actor (one liked the actor, the other did not). When asked what action each observer thought the actor was performing, both 6 and 8-year-olds correctly attributed negative interpretations to negatively biased observers and positive interpretations to positively biased observers. Four-year-olds responded randomly, despite remembering the information in the stories. Pillow and Henrichon (1996) reported similar results, but presented children with ambiguous restricted view pictures rather than ambiguous story events. Pillow and Mash (1999) conducted a direct comparison of children's attribution of false beliefs based on direct perceptual experience and false beliefs based on a biased interpretation of an ambiguous picture. Four and 5-year-olds accurately attributed false beliefs based on direct perception, but did not attribute false beliefs based on inferential or interpretive processes. This result supports the view that understanding differences in interpretation is distinct from understanding the possibility of false belief, with understanding of interpretive differences developing somewhat later. Lagatutta et al. (2010) found that as children become aware that observers with different past experiences may interpret ambiguous stimuli differently, children sometimes exaggerate differences in viewpoint. That is, 6–7-year-olds sometimes attributed different interpretations to observers with different past experiences even when the observers viewed informative, rather than ambiguous pictures, making differences in the observers' past experiences irrelevant for interpreting the pictures. Children's over-attribution of different viewpoints is consistent with a change in children's understanding of interpretative activity during the early elementary school years.

In some circumstances, children appear to understand interpretive processes before the age of six years. Barquero et al. (2003) reported that children as young as 5 years of age sometimes recognize that expectations may bias the interpretation of an ambiguous picture. For example, when told that an observer consistently likes drawings of houses and thinks any drawing is a picture of house, most 5, 6, and 7-year-olds responded that the observer would misinterpret a partially hidden drawing as being a picture of a house. However, children usually did not attribute a biased interpretation when an observer's expectation was based solely on past experience. Moreover, children often did not recognize that a naive observer might misinterpret an ambiguous portion of a partially hidden drawing. Although understanding of interpretive differences may begin around 5 years of age, children's understanding develops gradually and does not appear to be consistent across tasks and contexts until age 7 or 8 years. By 7 or 8 years of age children also recognize that self-interest may influence a person's construal of an event; however, children of this age typically regard self-interested interpretations of events as deliberate falsehoods, but by early adolescence children begin to recognize that bias may operate unconsciously (Mills and Keil 2005).

In addition to recognizing inference as a source of information, elementary school children learn to distinguish inferences from other thought processes. Six- and 7-year-olds distinguish problem solving based on reasoning from short cuts that do not involve reasoning, such as flipping a coin (Amsterlaw 2006). Six- and -seven-year-olds also distinguish deductive reasoning from guessing by rating deductive conclusions as more certain than arbitrary guesses (Pillow 2002; Pillow et al. 2000). Furthermore, 8–9-year-olds rate deductive inferences as more certain than inductive inferences, and 9–10-year-olds and adults rate inductions based on stronger evidence as more certain than inductions based on weaker evidence (Pillow and Pearson 2009). By late childhood or early adolescence children distinguish logically necessary inferences from invalid inferences (Miller et al. 2000; Morris 2000; Moshman and Franks 1986).

Young children sometimes have difficulty in recognizing ambiguity in evidence and determining what inferences a given pattern of information affords. For example, Pierraut-LeBonniec (1980) presented children with objects made either from straight sticks alone or from straight and curved sticks. Children also were shown a box containing only straight sticks and a box containing straight sticks and curved sticks. Then children were asked which box had been used to make each object. Because both boxes contained straight sticks, the object consisting of only straight sticks was an indeterminate problem: either box could have been used to construct it. The object made from straight and curved sticks was a determinate problem because only one box could have been used to construct it. Five-year-olds readily selected the correct box on determinate problems, but for indeterminate problems children almost always chose a specific box, as if they failed to recognize the indeterminacy of the evidence.

Subsequently, Fay and Klahr (1996) employed a similar procedure to question children more directly about the determinancy of evidence. Three types of construction pieces, straight sticks, curves, and squares were combined to create objects consisting of either: (a) straight sticks only, (b) curves only, (c) squares only, (d) straight sticks and curves, or (e) straight sticks and squares. Two boxes of construction pieces were presented along with each target object. For some problems (one vs. two feature), one box contained only one type of construction piece and the other box contained two types of pieces, including the type in the first box. For other problems (two vs. two feature), both boxes contained two types of pieces, with one type being included in both boxes and one type being unique to each box. Five-year-olds usually did not recognize indeterminacy on one vs. two feature problems, but performed somewhat better on two vs. two feature problems, reporting indeterminacy about half of the time. In a second experiment, children often overlooked indeterminacy on problems where the pieces in one box matched the target object and the other box was closed so that its contents were not visible. Fay and Klahr (1996) concluded that children often follow a positive capture rule. That is, when children identify a single matching box, they judge that they can tell which box was used to construct the target object. Klahr and Chen (2003) provided further evidence that 4 and 5-year-olds tend to use the positive capture strategy.

Examining children's ability to select an effective empirical test for deciding between two conflicting hypotheses, Sodian et al. (1991) found that children aged 6–9 years usually differentiated between a conclusive test and an inconclusive test. For example, in one experiment, children were told a story about two brothers who knew there was a mouse in their house, but had not observed it directly. The brothers had different beliefs about the size of the mouse. To determine whether the mouse was small or large, the brothers could either put out a box with a small opening containing food or box with a large opening containing food. Most children of all ages selected the box with the small opening, which provided conclusive evidence concerning whether the mouse was small enough to enter the box and eat the food. Thus, Sodian et al. (1991) argued that elementary school children can reason about what kind of evidence is conclusive for testing a hypothesis.

Studies of children's understanding of inference and children's evaluation of evidence indicate that preschool children often do not recognize the occurrence of inferences, preschool have difficulty in detecting ambiguity and recognizing the possibility of contrasting interpretations of evidence, and preschool children often do not appreciate the occurrence of biased interpretation. However, during the early elementary school years children begin to understand the occurrence of inference and interpretation.

2.1.1.5 Knowledge of Imagination

Attention, memory, inference, and interpretation typically are involved in processing and representing information about the world. Children also learn about cognitive activities, such as imagining or pretending, that generate representations not intended to reflect reality. Studies of children's understanding of pretending indicate that although 4-year-olds demonstrate understanding of pretending as a mental, rather than purely physical, activity in some circumstances (e.g., Joseph 1998; Sobel and Lillard 2001), children do not demonstrate consistent understanding pretending as a psychological process prior to 8 years of age (e.g., Lillard 1998). Young children differentiate between imaginary and real entities. Three- to five-year-old children appreciate that unlike real objects, imagined objects cannot be touched, cannot be seen by others, and do not persist over time (Wellman and Estes 1986). Children aged 3–5 years also regard the content of imagination as controllable, though belief in the controllability of imagination increases between 5 and 8 years of age (Woolley and Boerger 2002). Thus, awareness of imagination as deliberate activity that generates fictional mental states appears early in childhood. In contrast to other cognitive activities, such as selective attention, inference, or the stream of consciousness, children begin to learn about imagination at a relatively young age. Children's early knowledge of imagination may reflect its voluntary and effortful nature.

2.1.1.6 Knowledge About Relations Between Thought and Emotion

Because thoughts can trigger emotions and emotions likewise can trigger thoughts, understanding connections among cognitions and emotions is an important part of learning about cognitive activity. Research on children's understanding of emotion has examined (a) children's knowledge of emotional cuing, (b) children's understanding that an event may vary in emotional meaning for different individuals, (c) children's knowledge of thoughts accompanying emotional experiences such as guilt and (d) children's knowledge of emotional control strategies. Based on these studies, understanding of relations between thoughts and emotions appears to develop gradually from early childhood through late childhood.

Studies of emotional cuing indicate that some initial knowledge of links between thoughts and emotions appears during early childhood. Lagatutta et al. (1997) told children brief stories about a child story character who experienced a mildly sad event. At a later time and in happier circumstances, the story character encountered a cue associated with the earlier sad event. The story character then began to feel sad again. Children were asked to explain the story character's sadness. For example, in one story Mary's rabbit was chased away by dog with black spots. Several days later Mary felt sad again when her friend wanted her to play with his spotted puppy. Two types of explanations were of particular interest. Cognitive cuing responses explained that the character felt sad because seeing the cue led the character to think about the earlier sad event (e.g., "She thinks about her rabbit when she sees that puppy"). Cue responses explained that seeing the cue made the character sad, but did not mention thoughts about the prior sad event (e.g., "She's sad because she sees the dog."). Although 3-year-olds rarely gave cognitive cuing responses, they frequently gave cue responses, indicating some awareness of a connection between the cue and the character's emotion. Four-year-olds gave each type of response about half of the time, and 5-year-olds gave cognitive cuing responses, rather than cue responses, to the majority of stories. Thus, by 5 years of age children were able to articulate the link connecting past emotional experiences to currently present cue and current thoughts and emotions. In a subsequent study, Lagattuta and Wellman (2001) presented stories with characters who felt sad, angry, or happy following an initial event. At a later time, when the character encountered a cue associated with the initial event, the character felt an emotion congruent with that event rather than their present circumstances. Most 3, 4, and 5-year-olds explained the story character's emotion in terms of the past event. In addition, half of 3-year-olds and the majority of older children explained that the character's anger or sadness resulted from remembering the initial event. As was the case in the previous study, by age 5 the majority of children 'provided complete cognitive cuing responses.

Nonetheless, children's knowledge of the link between thought and emotion appears to be limited. In the absence of external cues related to an emotion, younger children do not necessarily invoke thoughts as a possible influence on emotional states. For instance, Flavell et al. (2001) reported that 8-year-olds and adults often explained a sudden change in emotion without any obvious external cause by appealing to the occurrence of emotionally significant thoughts, 5-year-olds did not. In addition, unlike 5-year-olds, older children and adults also suggested that thoughts can influence emotions (e.g., people can make themselves feel happy by thinking about something happy).

Prior to 8 years of age children also have difficulty in understanding individual differences in emotional responses to the same situation. For example, Gnepp and Gould (1985) investigated children's use of contextual information to make personalized inferences of emotion (i.e., using personal information about an individual to infer his or her emotional reaction to an event). When told about a prior event that could color a story character's response to a second event (e.g., a child's best friend previously said, "I don't like you anymore" and then the child saw the best friend on the playground), 10-year-olds and adults made personalized inferences about the character's emotions. That is, the older children and adults recognized that the prior event would influence the character's appraisal of the second event, which in turn would influence the character's emotional reaction to the second event (e.g., judging that the child would be sad when seeing the best friend because of thoughts about their falling out). Seven and eight-year-olds made personalized inferences much of the time, but not as often as older children, and 5-year-olds rarely made personalized inferences. Likewise, younger children often overlook information about an individual's personality traits when judging emotional reactions (Gnepp and Chilamkurti 1988).

Because complex emotions such as guilt, embarrassment, shame, or pride, involve characteristic combinations of affect and thought, full understanding of complex emotions entails some awareness of the intersection of emotion and cognition. Harris (1989) argues that even young children advance beyond a simple understanding of emotions as associated with or caused by particular situations.

Instead, according to Harris, by 4 years of age children understand emotions as derived from a person's desires and by 6 years children also view beliefs as consequential. For example, children were told that an elephant name Ellie only like to drink Coke and would not drink anything else. A monkey named Mickey emptied a Coke can and filled it with milk. (In an alternative version of the story, Mickey filled a milk container with Coke). Children were asked to predict Ellie's emotion both before and after discovering the contents of the can. Both 4-year-olds and 6-year-olds predicted that Ellie would feel sad upon discovering that a Coke can contained milk and would feel happy to find that a milk container held Coke. Furthermore, children's predictions were reversed when Ellie's favorite drink was milk. Thus, both age groups recognized that Ellie's response was mediated by her desire (Harris et al. 1989). However, before Ellie discovered the true contents of the misleading containers, 4 and 6-year-olds differed in their predictions. Six-year-olds based their predictions on Ellie's belief. They predicted she would feel happy when she, albeit mistakenly, believed the container held her preferred beverage and would feel sad when she believed it did not. In contrast, 4-year-olds over-looked Ellie's belief and predicted she would be happy whenever the container held her preferred drink, despite that fact that she thought otherwise.

Comprehending complex emotions presents an additional challenge beyond understanding that basic emotions such as happiness and sadness are mediated by mental states such as desires and beliefs. The experience of complex emotions depends upon one's sense of having met or failed to meet standards of behavior valued by the self and others. Thus, pride results not merely from achieving a desired outcome, but from awareness of personal responsibility for accomplishing a valued goal. Guilt occurs when one feels responsible for violating standards of moral behavior and deserving negative evaluations from self and others. Embarrassment and shame also reflect awareness of evaluation in terms of normative or moral standards. Younger children often do not appear to take account of personal responsibility or moral standards when predicting emotional responses. Thus, when judging a story character's pride or guilt, 5 and 6-year-olds do not differentiate between events with controllable versus uncontrollable outcomes (Graham 1988). In addition, 4 and 5-year-olds often predict that a child who victimizes another child, for example by taking the other child's possessions, will feel happy about the outcome, whereas 8-year-olds more often expect the victimizer to experience unpleasant emotions due to moral qualms (Arsenio Rivka 1992; Nunner-Winkler and Sodian 1988). As these results suggest, by approximately 8 years of age children recognize that emotional responses may be mediated by thoughts about violation of moral standards and responsibility for misdeeds. However, when provided information about at character's thoughts after the character had decided to break a rule, 4 and 5-year-olds predicted that a transgressor who was thinking about the rule or about possible negative outcomes felt worse compared to a transgressor who was thinking about the desire that motivated the transgression (Lagattuta 2008). Therefore, young children appear to be capable of thinking about diverse affective responses to a rule-violation, and young children also can reason about the link between thoughts and emotions.

Simultaneously inferring both the thoughts and the emotions that follow a trans-gression may be more challenging.

In addition to the relatively automatic effects of cognition on emotion, children also learn about deliberate strategies for controlling or managing their emotions. In a series of studies, Harris and colleagues interviewed children about their own strategies for controlling negative emotions (Harris 1989; Harris and Lipian 1989; Harris et al. 1981). From ages 6 to 15-years there were differences in the strategies children suggested. Six-year-olds, 10 and 11-year-olds, and 15-year-olds all mentioned coping with unhappiness by changing the situation, but children aged 10 or older were more likely to mention the possibility of redirecting their thoughts or engaging in a distracting activity. Thus, knowledge of cognitive strategies for deliberate control of emotion appears to increase in later childhood.

Research on children's understanding of emotion indicates that some awareness of the link between thoughts and feelings is apparent in early childhood, but knowledge of the relation between cognition and emotion increases in sophisti-cation at later ages. This research has examined children's understanding that thoughts can influence emotions. Children's awareness of the reciprocal possi-bility, that emotions can influence thoughts, appears to have received little attention. However, Flavell et al. (2001) reported that 8-year-olds and adults, but not 5-year-olds, recognized that a person who is feeling sad also is likely to be thinking sad thoughts. Children's understanding of bidirectional influence between thoughts and emotions remains to be investigated. Although understanding of the connection between cognition and emotion appears to develop gradually into late childhood and adolescence, young children's knowledge of cognitive cuing of emotion is noteworthy. The salience and personal significance of affective states may enhance awareness of situations and thoughts associated with them, thereby facilitating early learning about emotional cues and their consequences.

2.1.1.7 Knowledge About the Controllability of Thoughts

As children learn about cognitive processes such as attention, memory, and rea-soning, they also learn about some general characteristics of cognitive activity. Controllability is one such characteristic. Theories of cognition often distinguish between controlled processes and automatic processes (e.g., Hasher and Zacks 1979). Controlled processes require attention, and thus are more effortful and are subject to deliberate conscious control. Automatic processes can be performed without allocating attention to them, and they may occur outside of consciousness and may be involuntary or not directly controllable. Intuitions about the control-lability of mental states are included in older children's and adults' naive theories of mental functioning. Children know about the occurrence of both controlled processes, such as deliberate memory strategies, and automatic processes, such as cognitive and emotional cuing during the elementary school years, but knowledge about the controllability (and especially, uncontrollability) of mental states develops relatively late. For example, Flavell et al. (1998) found that 13-year-olds and adults were more likely than 5 and 9-year-olds to recognize that upon seeing a shot needle, a child awaiting a shot would automatically think about receiving an injection or that a child who hears a strange noise would wonder about it, even if these children did not want to think about anything. They also found that older children and adults were more likely than 5-year-olds to judge that a person could not go three days without thinking about anything. Flavell and Green (1999) investigated children's and adults' intuitions about the ability to intentionally cease various mental states. Seven-year-olds, 10-year-olds, and adults were presented with examples of mental states that should be hard to extinguish deliberately (e.g., a strong desire or a strong fear) or easy to change (e.g., a visual fixation or the content of imagination). Although even the 7-year-olds judged some mental states as harder to control than others, 10-year-olds and adults more clearly distinguished the hard to control states from the easy to control states.

Pillow and Pearson (2011) investigated children's and adults' judgments about the controllability of four processes, object recognition, deductive inference, interpretive inference, and pretending. First-grade, third-grade, and fifth-grade children and adults engaged in each of these tasks and then, using a five-point scale, rated how easy it would be to think of an alternative outcome for each task. For object recognition, participants saw a picture of an elephant, and were asked: "When you looked at the picture, did you have to see an elephant or could you see a giraffe instead? Show me with the arrow. Put the arrow here if it would be very easy. Put the arrow here if it would be very hard, and put the arrow here if it would be very easy". For the deduction task, participants saw a toy car and a toy dinosaur. After they were hidden in separate containers, participants viewed one toy and were asked what toy was in the other container. Then they rated how hard it would be to think the other alternative was in the container. For interpretive inference, participants viewed a sequence of three pictures of the same type (e.g., three sharks). While viewing a small ambiguous portion of a fourth picture (e.g., a triangle seen through an aperture), they were asked to identify it (typically, as a shark). Then participants rated the difficulty of thinking the fourth picture was something else. For the pretend trial, participants were asked to pretend there was something in an empty box, and then rated the difficulty of pretending something else. Because object recognition is automatic and pretend is controlled, those tasks provided standards for comparison. If participants distinguished between automatic and controlled tasks, they should give high difficulty ratings for object recognition (i.e., judging that is difficult to look at an elephant and voluntarily see a giraffe) and low difficulty ratings for pretend (i.e., judging that it is easy to pretend various things are in an empty box). Although first-grade children did not distinguish among the four tasks in their ratings, third- and fifth-grade children gave higher ratings for object recognition than for either interpretive inference or pretend. Adults gave higher ratings for object recognition and deductive inference, compared to interpretive inference or pretend. Thus, a distinction between automatic and controlled processes is evident among adults and appears to emerge as early as third grade.

2.1.2 Organizational Knowledge

As children acquire knowledge of the occurrence, function, and characteristics of specific cognitive activities, they develop the potential to reflect on, compare, and organize these psychological concepts. Organizational knowledge refers to beliefs about functional relations, similarities, and differences among cognitive activities. During early childhood, knowledge of mental functioning is organized in terms of relations among beliefs, desires, action, and perception, and during middle childhood this simple belief-desire reasoning begins to be elaborated into a conception of the mind as an active information processor, in which children understand that processes such as reasoning, remembering, learning, and imagining contribute to the formation of beliefs (e.g.,Chandler 1987; Wellman 1990). By late childhood, having acquired knowledge of the occurrence of cognitive activities, children begin to organize this knowledge in terms of similarities in the characteristics and functions of different cognitive processes (e.g., Schwanenflugel et al. 1998). Because organizational knowledge represents recognition of the mind as an information-processing entity, such knowledge potentially provides a foundation for thinking about the origin and nature of knowledge in general. In this section, research on the organization of children's concepts of cognitive activities is reviewed. This research suggests that between middle childhood and adulthood, concepts of cognition are increasingly organized in terms of features such as the reception of input or the generation of output, degree of certainty, memory, attentional, and inferential demands, and deliberate effortful processing.

Schwanenflugel and Fabricius and their colleagues have investigated developmental changes in the organization of concepts of cognition by examining children's and adults' judgments of similarity among cognitive activities. In two studies, 8-year-olds, 10-year-olds, and adults rated the similarity of how their mind is used in a variety of activities, such as "learning a new board game from the instructions on the box" (comprehension), "saying happy birthday on the right day to your friend who told you her birthday a long time ago" (memory), "listening to announcements being made a lunch time in a noisy cafeteria" (attention), "knowing that your mother baked cookies for your school party by seeing the dirty dishes" (inference), etc. (Fabricius et al. 1989; Schwanenflugel et al. 1994). Over this age range, multidimensional scaling analyses indicated an increased emphasis on similarities in the cognitive processing demands, as opposed to more superficial features, of the tasks. For example, Schwanenflugel et al. (1994) found that adults organized the activities primarily in terms of a memory dimension, reflecting whether or not memory was a major component of an activity (e.g., list memory and prospective memory vs. attention or inference), and also used an inference dimension (e.g., inference and recognition vs. attention and planning) and an attention dimension (e.g., attention and comparison vs. planning and comprehension). Ten-year-old children organized the activities in terms of a memory dimension primarily, and also included an attention dimension and a planning dimension (e.g., planning and prospective memory vs. comprehension and inference). In contrast, 8-year-olds organized the activities mainly in terms of whether they involved going somewhere or staying in one place and whether the activity was something the individual wants to do or something someone else wants the individual to do. Eight-year-olds also organized items in terms of whether they required memory, but this dimension played a weaker role in their similarity ratings compared to adults' ratings. Fabricius et al. (1989) did not find evidence for a memory dimension in 8-year-olds' ratings. Instead, in that study, 8-year-olds judged similarity mainly in terms of sensory features of the tasks, such as the degree to which they involved seeing or hearing.

In two further studies, children and adults were asked to rate the similarity of pairs of mental verbs (e.g., know, understand, think, guess, memorize, notice, explain, etc.) in terms of how the mind is used in the activities referred to by each verb (Schwanenflugel et al. 1996, 1998). Schwanenflugel et al. (1996) reported that two major dimensions emerged in multidimensional scaling analyses of similarity ratings by children and adults: information-processing and certainty. The information-processing dimension ranged from perceptual processing of input (e.g., hear, attend, notice) to production of output (e.g., decide, invent), with processes that mediate between the two near the middle of the dimension (e.g., think, memorize). The certainty dimension ranged from verbs implying high certainty at one end (e.g., know, understand, memorize) to those indicating less certainty in the middle (e.g., think) and those indicating low certainty at the opposite end (e.g., guess). Both dimensions appeared in the multidimensional scaling solutions for 8-year-olds, 10-year-olds, and adults; however, the relative weights of these dimensions changed with age. Children emphasized information-processing more than certainty, and adults emphasized certainty more. Also, adults weighted certainty more heavily than did children. Schwanenflugel et al. (1998) reported a similar pattern of results. They presented children and adults with a list of mental verbs and a set of scenarios depicting different mental activities. For each scenario, participants were asked to select all of the verbs that described how they would use their minds in that situation. As in the previous study, the verbs were organized in terms of certainty and information-processing dimensions, and adults emphasized certainty more than did 8 or 10-year-olds.

By adulthood further refinements appear in the organization of psychological concepts. Schwanenflugel et al. (1994) found that adults distinguished recall from recognition memory, and divided recall into list memory and prospective memory. In addition, Parault and Schwanenflugel (2000) reported that adults distinguish varieties of attention. Similarity judgments indicated that adults treat attentional orienting (automatic attention to salient events), divided attention (monitoring two sources at once), perceptual comparison (intermittently sampling and comparing multiple pieces of information), and attentional inhibition (suppressing a behavior) as distinct categories of cognitive activity. Adults also organized attentional activities along an effort dimension, with voluntary, effortful concentration at one end and automatic attentional orienting at the other end.

Schwanenflugel et al. (1994, 1998) argue that the organizational changes documented in this program of research demonstrate that an understanding of constructive processing develops during middle childhood. That is, during middle childhood there is growing awareness of inferential and interpretive activities, accompanied by the realization that cognitive activities differ in certainty, with activities that are highly inferential or based on little information being less certain. Compared to children, adults are more aware of the selective nature of attention and information-processing. As children's understanding of the occurrence of cognitive activities becomes elaborated and organized, a more abstract, conception of the mind emerges. Children progress beyond an initial recognition of specific cognitive events toward a more general conception of thinking. Moshman's (1998) distinction between inference and thinking provides insight into this metacognitive change. According to Moshman, inference is a process of generating new cognitions from old cognitions, and thinking consists of the deliberate coordination of inferences to serve purposes such as planning, problem solving, decision-making, etc. As children develop an understanding of thinking, they come to view cognitive acts as organized, systematic, and purposeful, rather than as separate occurrences of specific activities. Viewing thought in terms of deliberately related cognitive acts implies knowledge of the mind as organized processor of information. Schwanenflugel et al. (1994) suggest that children's subjective experiences of uncertainty and ambiguity help to motivate the building of this constructive theory of mind.

2.1.3 Epistemological Thought and Metacognitive Theories

The understanding of cognitive activities that emerges from middle childhood through adolescence constitutes an important advancement in children's appreciation of subjectivity. Although some understanding of subjectivity appears early in childhood, this understanding is limited. For example, 4 and 5-year-olds understand that another person may hold a mistaken belief (e.g., Wimmer and Perner 1983). This early understanding is limited to recognition that differences in individuals' objective circumstances (i.e., witnessing different events) can produce differences in subjective states. By 7 years of age children begin to recognize that psychological processes contribute to the creation of subjective differences, as evidenced by children's understanding of differences in interpretation (e.g., Carpendale and Chandler 1996; Pillow and Henrichon 1996). At this age understanding of subjectivity also remains limited. Chandler (1987) distinguished between a case-specific understanding of interpretive differences and a more general understanding of knowledge as inherently constructive. A case-specific understanding, of the sort demonstrated by 7-year-olds, refers to the ability to recognition that a specific piece of ambiguous information may be misinterpreted by a naive or biased observer. In contrast, a general understanding of the mind as constructive entails recognition of the pervasive role of psychological processes in the formation of knowledge and beliefs. According to Kuhn et al. (1988), appreciation of interpretive activity as an inherent part of knowledge begins to emerge during adolescence, but often does not develop until adulthood. In this section, three theoretical perspectives on epistemological development are described and some empirical findings concerning age-related changes in epistemological thought are briefly summarized.

Together, the occurrence knowledge of cognitive activities that develops during middle childhood and the organizational knowledge that begins in late childhood may provide a foundation for more advanced epistemological thought during adolescence. As older children and adolescents increasingly organize their knowledge of cognitive activities in terms of concepts of information-processing and certainty (e.g. Schwanenflugel et al. 1996) and distinguish between theory and evidence (e.g., Koslowski 1996; Kuhn et al. 1995), they may glean general insights concerning the relationship between the mind and the world. Such reflections may lead to a new appreciation of subjectivity. Thus, Schraw and Moshman (1995) argued that from late childhood through adolescence, children gradually consolidate their knowledge of cognition and integrate it with cognitive monitoring. Through this process they construct metacognitive theories; that is, a systematized framework of knowledge about cognition that can be used to predict and explain events. Schraw and Moshman distinguish systematic metacognitive theories from earlier developing, but not yet systematized, knowledge of specific cognitive processes, or metacognitive knowledge.

The notion that adolescents and adults develop an increasingly systematic and abstract view of the mind and knowledge is central to theories of epistemological development. In response to college students' course evaluations, Perry (1970) conducted a longitudinal study of students' views of knowledge, intellectual authority, and education, interviewing students at the end of each of their four years of college. Based on this study, Perry (1970) proposed a developmental progression in epistemological thought during late adolescence and early adulthood. Perry (1970) suggested many first year college students take a strongly objectivist view of knowledge, which assumes that correct answers exist for all questions and are known by authorities. As they progress through college, students typically come to view knowledge as subjective, recognizing that because even the authorities' knowledge remains incomplete, differences of opinion exist. Moreover, some individuals take the strongly subjectivist stance that, in the absence of certain authoritative knowledge, all opinions are equally valid and merely a matter of preference. By the end of four years of college, Perry found a more complex view of knowledge becoming increasingly common. While continuing to assume that all knowledge is relative, some students also recognized that opinions are derived from evidence and reasoning. Instead of all opinions being equally valid, differing opinions, and the evidence and reasoning supporting them, can be evaluated, with the result that some views may be judged more plausible than others. Moshman (2005) has termed this progression of epistemological stances objectivist, subjectivist, and rationalist epistemology.

Following Perry's pioneering work, several theories of epistemological thought have been proposed and a large body of empirical research has been conducted (for reviews see King and Kitchener 1994; Hofer and Pintrich 2002). The general progression from objectivist epistemology to subjectivist, and then rationalist, epistemology has continued to be a central theme in many more recent theoretical frameworks (e.g., Chandler 1987; King and Kitchener 1994; Kuhn et al. 1988; Moshman 2005). In their influential seven stage model, Kitchener and King (1981) proposed stages characterized by the assumption knowledge is objective and complete (Stage 1), the assumption that knowledge is inherently uncertain and opinions are personal preferences (Stage 4) and the assumption that viewpoints can be evaluated in terms of the evidence and reasoning supporting them (Stages 6 and 7). Both cross-sectional and longitudinal studies indicate that progress through these stages occurs gradually during adolescence and adulthood, with stage of reasoning being correlated with both age and education (e.g., King and Kitchener 1994).

In their examination of the development scientific thinking and epistemology, Kuhn et al. (1988) identified a progression in adolescents' and adults' reasoning about the relation between theory and evidence which roughly parallels the stages proposed by Perry (1970) and King and Kitchener (1994). For example, in one study they assessed participants' understanding of discrepant accounts of a fictitious war provided by historians from each of the opposing sides. Level 0 participants viewed accounts of historical events as accurate statements of fact, whereas at Levels 1 and 2 participants recognized that historical accounts could be incomplete, but across these first three levels of epistemological thinking, participants did not realize that accounts could be interpretations that differ from the events they describe. Awareness of interpretive differences between historical accounts emerged in Level 3, but these discrepancies were regarded as equally valid differences in opinion. Level 4 thinking treated differences in interpretation as differences in emphasis, rather than as constructions based on different world views. At Level 5 knowledge was recognized as the inherently subjective product of interpretive processes that are entrenched within cultural belief systems. Participants' level of reasoning increased with age and education level from early adolescence through adulthood. During sixth-grade children's responses ranged from Level 0 to Level 2. Some adolescents provided Level 3 responses in ninth-grade, but most responded at Levels 1 or Level 2. Level 4 and 5 responses first appeared during twelfth-grade and became somewhat more frequent during adulthood; however Level 5 responses remained rare among both non-student adults and graduate students. More recently, Kuhn (2001) has distinguished among three levels of epistemological thought: absolutist, multiplist, and evaluativist. These three levels generally parallel Moshman's objectivist, subjectivist, and rationalist epistemologies. Kuhn (2001) proposes that a multiplist conception of knowledge is most likely to emerge during adolescence, but an evaluativist conception develops gradually, over a period of years, and so may be achieved later.

The studies reported by Perry (1970), Kitchener and King (1981), and Kuhn et al. (1988) indicate that rationalist thought develops primarily during adulthood. Substantial individual differences were reported in all three studies, and the most advanced levels of epistemological thought may be relatively infrequent. For instance, Thoermer and Sodian (2002) reported that in interviews with both first year undergraduate students and advanced graduate students pursuing degrees in biology, chemistry, or physics, explicit discussion of the influence of theories on the interpretation of data was rare. In contrast, Clinchy et al. (1977) found rationalist thought among students in their senior year at a progressive high school that encouraged critical thinking. Questioning adolescents about issues relevant to their own experience (e.g., whether 16-year-olds are sufficiently responsible to drive), Chandler et al. (1990) found an increase in rationalist thinking, which they term post skeptical rationalism, from eight to twelfth-grade.

Beliefs about the origin of different viewpoints and the importance of evidence for resolving disagreements appear to vary according to both age and the type of issue in question (Robinson and Apperly 1998; Rowley and Robinson 2002). For example, Rowley and Robinson (2002) investigated adolescents' and adults' explanations of differences in the interpretation of evidence. Adolescents and adults were presented with a value-laden dispute and a scientific dispute. The value-laden dispute was a disagreement between parents and students about whether a drivers' education course should be offered at a hypothetical high school. The scientific dispute concerned the cause of a skin disease. In each case, the opposing views were based on limited sample of evidence. All age groups, 13–15 year olds, 16–17 year olds, 18–20 year olds, and 40–60 year olds, recognized the possibility that individuals could interpret the same sample of evidence in different ways. In addition, participants of all ages also explained the value-laden dispute as reflecting internal psychological factors, i.e., differences in pre-existing biases, opinions, and motives, and all age groups agreed that additional evidence would not be helpful in resolving the disagreement. Adolescents and adults differed in the views regarding the scientific dispute. Adults, aged 18–20 and 40–60, typically attributed the disagreement to insufficient evidence, an external factor, and judged that additional evidence would be effective for changing views about the cause of the skin disease. In contrast, younger adolescents, 13–15-year-olds, were more likely emphasize internal psychological factors as the explanation for the dispute and less likely to view additional evidence as effective for resolving the disagreement. Thus, overall adolescents discriminated less between the two types of disputes than did adults.

Individual differences in epistemological values influence reasoning. Klacyznski (2000) investigated biases in adolescents' reasoning. Adolescents were asked to evaluate evidence relevant to their beliefs about relations between either social class or religion and variables such as parenting, morality, and satisfaction with life. When reasoning about social class or religion, adolescents used more sophisticated scientific reasoning strategies when rejecting evidence that was inconsistent with their prior theories, and made more superficial heuristic judgments when evaluating evidence that was consistent with their prior theories. Moreover, adolescents' theories became more extreme or polarized following presentation of evidence. However, both of these effects were influenced by adolescents' epistemological attitudes. Measures of four aspects of adolescents' epistemological dispositions were combined into an overall epistemological disposition score. The four measures assessed enjoyment of intellectual challenges,

openness to revising beliefs, tendencies to avoid uncertainty, contradictory prop-
ositions, or ill-defined problems, and reliance on rationality rather than intuition.
Composite epistemological disposition scores moderated both reasoning biases
and belief polarization. Thus, adolescents who were more "knowledge-driven",
or open to uncertainty, consideration of other views, etc., were more likely to use
sophisticated scientific reasoning, less likely to use biased reasoning, and less
likely to polarize their beliefs compared to adolescents who were more "belief-
driven".

Although similarities and differences among the forms of subjectivist and
rationalist thought documented in adolescence and adulthood remain to be clarified
(Chandler et al. 2002), research on epistemological development indicates that
increasingly sophisticated views of mental activity emerge across this age span.
For many adolescents and adults, recognition of subjective psychological states
and processes has implications for views of the nature of knowledge and the
relation between the mind and reality. Moreover, in addition to age-related
changes, individual differences in epistemological thought emerge during adolescence and remain important through adulthood.

2.2 Developmental Trends

In reviewing research on children's understanding of cognition, I have distinguished among knowledge of the occurrence of particular cognitive activities,
knowledge of the organization of cognitive activities, and more abstract epistemological thought about the nature of knowledge, mind, and reality. As these
distinctions imply, with increased age the content of children's knowledge about
cognition may grow more elaborate and abstract. In addition, as suggested
by Schraw and Moshman (1995), there also may be a trend toward increasingly
explicit understanding of cognition. Each of these trends will be discussed briefly
below.

Several theorists have proposed developmental changes in the generality of
children's metacognitive knowledge. As mentioned earlier, Chandler (1987)
suggested that children's initial understanding of interpretive processes is case-
specific. In a particular instance, children may recognize that an observer may
misinterpret ambiguous information. However, this momentary recognition occurs
on a case-by-case basis and is not yet integrated into a general view of knowledge
as constructed through cognitive activity. Similarly, Schraw and Moshman (1995)
distinguished metacognitive knowledge and metacognitive theories. Metacognitive
knowledge includes declarative knowledge about cognitive processes, whereas
metacognitive theories are broader frameworks constructed to systematize such
knowledge and achieve a more formal understanding of cognitive activities. The
basic understanding of cognitive activities that I have termed occurrence knowledge may begin as case-specific knowledge of particular cognitive phenomena.
Children may begin by noticing instances of remembering, forgetting, attending

selectively, or making inferences, etc. As experience with a particular type of cognitive event accumulates, children may begin to conceptualize that process, with knowledge of individual cognitive activities remaining relatively isolated at first. Eventually children may begin to notice similarities and differences among cognitive activities, perhaps involving their functions or the contexts in which they occur. Gradually children may begin to represent, at least implicitly, features or dimensions along which cognitive activities may be compared, and knowledge of the organization of cognitive activities emerges. During middle childhood knowledge of cognitive activities becomes organized in terms of their input–output functions and their associated level of certainty (Schwanenflugel et al. 1994, 1998). According to Schwanenflugel and colleagues, the development of this organizational framework marks the appearance of a more general understanding of the mind as a constructive processor of information. Although some recognition of subjectivity can be seen in early childhood; for example, in young children's understanding of differences in beliefs, older children's increased awareness of constructive activities lays the groundwork for a more general confrontation with subjectivity. During adolescence the objectivity versus subjectivity of knowledge becomes a central issue of epistemological reflection.

I have proposed that occurrence knowledge, organizational knowledge, and epistemological thought form a developmental progression, but these levels of understanding do not constitute distinct stages. Instead, they may overlap each other, with one level beginning to emerge while the previous levels continue to develop. Moreover, these three levels of understanding may influence each other bidirectionally. For instance, accumulating occurrence knowledge may create an informational base that, by allowing comparison and analysis, facilitates the development of organizational knowledge. At the same time, organizational knowledge may help children acquire new knowledge about the occurrence of cognitive activities or help them refine, revise, or elaborate prior knowledge. Likewise, in middle and late childhood the development of organizational knowledge may be a step toward adolescent epistemological thought, but in turn epistemological reflection may result in new insights into both the organization of cognitive functioning and the occurrence of specific cognitive activities.

In addition to changes in the organization and abstractness of knowledge about cognition, there also may be changes in the explicitness of children's understanding. Schraw and Moshman (1995) identified three types of metacognitive theories: (a) tacit theories, (b) explicit informal theories, and (c) explicit formal theories. Tacit theories are held without any explicit awareness of possessing a theory. Tacit theories are implicit organizational frameworks that serve to organize knowledge and that may affect behavior and decision-making. Schraw and Moshman suggest that because an individual is not explicitly aware of either the theory or evidence that supports or refutes the theory, tacit theories are not easily distinguished from evidence or tested against data. Informal theories include some explicit knowledge, but are fragmentary, with individuals being aware of some of the assumptions that comprise the theory without having formed an explicit, integrated theoretical framework. Having at least some explicit awareness of their assumptions enables individuals to distinguish the content of their theory from the data the theory attempts to explain. With this distinction, it becomes possible to evaluate and modify metacognitive theories. Explicit formal theories are highly systematic and explicit explanatory structures of the sort created by experts and taught in advanced academic settings. Schraw and Moshman note that explicit formal theories are rare and typically are limited to an individual's immediate area of expertise when they do occur. Therefore, it seems likely that most children and adults do not develop full explicit formal theories of cognitive functioning, but may achieve informal theories. More generally, Karmiloff-Smith (1996) has characterized development within cognitive domains as a process of constructing increasingly explicit representations, such that initially implicit procedures become objects of thought that can be compared and eventually accessed into consciousness.

These two developmental trends, the progression from occurrence knowledge to organizational knowledge and epistemological reflection, and the progression toward increasingly explicit knowledge, can be viewed as intertwined. Knowledge of the occurrence of particular cognitive events and activities may begin as case-specific, non-theoretical, and implicit. Over time this knowledge may become more general and explicit. As a result, children come to have concepts of cognitive activities, such as attention, memory, reasoning, the stream of consciousness, etc. Increased explicitness may facilitate the construction of organizational knowledge. At first organizational knowledge represents a tacit theory, but with increased explicitation may form the basis for an informal explicit theory. Because informal theories are amenable to evaluation and revision, possession of an informal theory of cognitive functioning would enable epistemological reflection and further theorizing.

2.3 Summary

Between preschool and adolescence, children progress from a basic understanding of mental states to understanding of some properties of cognitive activities such as attention, memory, and inference, and then to epistemological reflection on the nature of human knowledge. Kuhn (2000) suggests that young children's understanding of beliefs provides a foundation for further epistemological development. The present model distinguishes mental state reasoning and three aspects of conceptual knowledge of cognitive activities: Occurrence knowledge, organizational knowledge, and epistemological reflection. These three aspects of conceptual understanding may form a developmental progression, with occurrence knowledge providing a foundation for the development of organizational knowledge and in turn being further refined as organizational knowledge develops. Organizational knowledge represents implicit recognition of the mind as a systematic entity. This recognition of the mind as a system of subjective states and processes may facilitate thinking about the relation between the mind and external reality, a core concern in the development of an epistemological framework. However, occurrence knowledge of cognitive activities, organizational knowledge, and epistemological reflection have been investigated separately. Developmental relations among mental state understanding, occurrence knowledge of cognitive activities, organizational knowledge of cognitive activities, and epistemological reflection remain to be determined empirically.

In this chapter I primarily have discussed descriptive research concerning age-related patterns in children's knowledge of cognitive functioning. Describing age-related changes is an important endeavor and one of my goals, but the patterns of change described here pose an explanatory question: How do such changes occur? That is, how do children learn about cognition? To address this question, I will consider possible sources of information about cognitive activity and also discuss possible learning mechanisms. Research concerning children's conceptual knowledge of cognitive activities has described age-related changes in children's understanding of cognitive functioning, but typically has not examined mechanisms of knowledge acquisition or modification. A more complete picture of development could be achieved by integrating studies of age-related changes in children's knowledge of cognitive activities with investigation of children's monitoring of phenomenological experience and children's participation in the social construction of knowledge about cognitive functioning. Research on the development of cognitive monitoring is reviewed next in Chap. 4, followed by a discussion of social influences on children's understanding of mental functioning in Chap. 5. Then in Chap. 6 I attempt to integrate cognitive monitoring, social experience, and conceptual understanding of cognition, and I also consider learning processes that may contribute to the development of metacognitive knowledge.

References

Amsterlaw, J. (2006). Children's beliefs about everyday reasoning. *Child Development, 77*, 443–464.

Arsenio, W. R., & Rivka, K. (1992). Victimizers and their victims: Children's conception of the mixed emotional consequences of moral transgressions. *Child Development, 63*, 915–927.

Astington, J. (1993). *The child's discovery of the mind*. Cambridge: Harvard University Press.

Barquero, B., Robinson, E. J., & Thomas, G. V. (2003). Children's ability to attribute different interpretations of ambiguous drawings to a naive vs. a biased observer. *International Journal of Behavioral Development, 27*, 445–456.

Bartsch, K., & Wellman, H. M. (1989). Young children's attribution of action to beliefs and desires. *Child Development, 60*, 946–964.

Bartsch, K., & Wellman, H. M. (1995). Children talk about the mind. New York: Oxford University Press.

Beal, C. R. (1985). Development of knowledge about the use of cues to aid prospective retrieval. *Child Development, 56*, 631–642.

Beal, C. R., & Flavell, J. H. (1983). Young speakers' evaluation of their listener's comprehension in a referential communication task. *Child Development, 54*, 148–153.

Broughton, J. (1978). Development of concepts of self, mind, reality, and knowledge. *New Directions for Child and Adolescent Development, 1*, 75–100.

Carey, S., & Smith, C. (1993). On understanding the nature of scientific knowledge. *Educational Psychologist, 28*, 235–251.

Carpendale, J. I., & Chandler, M. J. (1996). On the distinction between false belief understanding and subscribing to an interpretative theory of mind. *Child Development, 67*, 1686–1706.

Chandler, M. J. (1987). The Othello effect: essay on the emergence and eclipse of skeptical doubt. *Human Development, 30*, 137–159.

Chandler, M. J. (1988). Doubt and developing theories of mind. In J. W. Astington, P. L. Harris, & D. R. Olson (Eds.), *Developing theories of mind* (pp. 387–413). New York: Cambridge University Press.

Chandler, M. J., & Boyes, M. (1982). Social cognitive development. In B. B. Wolman (Ed.), *Handbook of developmental psychology* (pp. 387–402). New.Jersey: Prentice-Hall.

Chandler, M., & Helm, D. (1984). Developmental changes in the contribution of shared experience to social role-taking competence. *International Journal of Behavioral Development, 7*, 145–156.

Chandler, M. J., Boyes, M., & Ball, L. (1990). Relativism and stations of epistemic doubt. *Journal of Experimental Child Psychology, 50*, 370–395.

Chandler, M. J., Hallett, D., & Sokol, B. W. (2002). Competing claims about competing knowledge claims. In B. K. Hofer & P. R. Pintrich (Eds.), *Personal epistemology: The psychology of beliefs about knowledge and knowing* (pp. 145–168). New Jersey: Lawrence Erlbaum Associates.

Clinchy, B., Lief, J., & Young, P. (1977). Epistemological and moral development in girls from a traditional and a progressive high school. *Journal of Educational Psychology, 69*, 337–343.

Dunn, J. (1999). Making sense of the social world: Mindreading, emotion, and relationships. In P. D. Zelazo, J. W. Astington, & D. R. Olson (Eds.), *Developing theories of intention: Social understanding and self-control* (pp. 229–242). New Jersey: Lawrence Erlbaum Associates.

Fabricius, W. V., Schwanenflugel, P. J., Kyllonen, P. C., Barclay, C. R., & Denton, S. M. (1989). Developing theories of mind: children's and adult's concepts of mental activities. *Child Development, 60*, 1278–1290.

Fay, A. L., & Klahr, D. (1996). Knowing about guessing and guessing about knowing: preschoolers' understanding of indeterminacy. *Child Development, 67*, 689–716.

Flavell, J. H., & Green, F. L. (1999). Development of intuitions about the controllability of different mental states. *Cognitive Development, 14*, 133–146.

Flavell, J. H., & Miller, P. H. (1998). Social cognition. In W. Damon, D. Kuhn, & R. S. Siegler (Eds.), *Handbook of child psychology: Vol. 2. Cognition, perception, and language* (5th ed., pp. 851–898). New Jersey: Wiley.

Flavell, J. H., Shipstead, S. G., & Croft, K. (1978). Young children's knowledge about visual perception: hiding objects from others. *Child Development, 49*, 1208–1211.

Flavell, J. H., Green, F. L., & Flavell, E. R. (1993). Children's understanding of the stream of consciousness. *Child Development, 64*, 387–398.

Flavell, J. H., Green, F. L., & Flavell, E. R. (1995). The development of children's knowledge about attentional focus. *Developmental Psychology, 31*, 706–712.

Flavell, J. H., Green, F. L., Flavell, E. R., & Grossman, J. B. (1997). The development of children's knowledge about inner speech. *Child Development, 68*, 39–47.

Flavell, J. H., Green, F. L., & Flavell, E. R. (1998). The mind has a mind of its own: developing knowledge about mental uncontrollability. *Cognitive Development, 13*, 127–138.

Flavell, J. H., Flavell, E. R., & Green, F. L. (2001). Development of children's understanding of connections between thinking and feeling. *Psychological Science, 12*, 430–432.

Gnepp, J., & Chilamkurti, C. (1988). Children's use of personality attributions to predict other people's emotional and behavioral reactions. *Child Development, 59*, 743–754.

Gnepp, J., & Gould, M. E. (1985). The development of personalized inferences: understanding other people's emotional reactions in light of their prior experiences. *Child Development, 56*, 1455–1464.

Gordon, F. R., & Flavell, J. H. (1977). The development of intuitions about cognitive cueing. *Child Development, 48*, 1027–1033.

Graham, S. (1988). Children's developing understanding of the motivational role of affect: an attributional analysis. *Cognitive Development, 3,* 71–88.

Harris, P. L. (1989). *Children and emotion.* Oxford: Blackwell Publishing.

Harris, P. L., & Lipian, M. (1989). Understanding emotion and experiencing emotion. In C. Saarni & P. L. Harris (Eds.), *Children's understanding of emotion* (pp. 241–258). New York: Cambridge University Press.

Harris, P. L., Olthof, T., & Terwogt, M. M. (1981). Children's knowledge of emotion. *Journal of Child Psychology and Psychiatry, 22,* 247–261.

Harris, P. L., Johnson, C. N., Hutton, D., Andrews, G., & Cooke, T. (1989). Young children's theory of mind and emotion. *Cognition and Emotion, 3,* 379–400.

Hasher, L., & Zacks, R. T. (1979). Automatic and effortful processes in memory. *Journal of Experimental Psychology: General, 108,* 356–388.

Higgins, E. T. (1981). Role taking and social judgment: Alternative developmental perspectives and processes. In J. H. Flavell & L. Ross (Eds.), *Social cognitive development: Frontiers and possible futures* (pp. 119–153). Cambridge: Cambridge University Press.

Hofer, B. K., & Pintrich, P. R. (2002). *Personal epistemology: The psychology of beliefs about knowledge and knowing.* New Jersey: Lawrence Erlbaum Associates.

Hogrefe, G. J., Wimmer, H., & Perner, J. (1986). Ignorance versus false belief: a developmental lag in the attribution of epistemic states. *Child Development, 57,* 567–582.

Joseph, R. M. (1998). Intention and knowledge in preschoolers' conception of pretend. *Child Development, 69,* 966–980.

Justice, E. M. (1985). Categorization as a preferred memory strategy: developmental changes during elementary school. *Developmental Psychology, 21,* 1105–1110.

Justice, E. M. (1986). Developmental changes in judgements of relative strategy effectiveness. *British Journal of Developmental Psychology, 4,* 75–81.

Karmiloff-Smith, A. (1996). *Beyond modularity: A developmental perspective on cognitive science.* Cambridge, MA: MIT Press.

Keenan, T. R., Ruffman, T., & Olson, D. R. (1994). When do children begin to understand logical inference as a source of knowledge? *Cognitive Development, 9,* 331–353.

King, P. M., & Kitchener, K. (1994). *Developing reflective judgment: Understanding and promoting intellectual growth and critical thinking in adolescents and adults.* San Francisco: Jossey-Bass.

Kitchener, K. S., & King, P. M. (1981). Reflective judgment: concepts of justification and their relationship to age and education. *Journal of Applied Developmental Psychology, 2,* 89–116.

Klacyznski, P. (2000). Motivated scientific reasoning biases, epistemological beliefs, and theory polarization: A two-process approach to adolescent cognition. *Child Development, 71,* 1347–1366.

Klahr, D., & Chen, Z. (2003). Overcoming the positive-capture strategy in young children: learning about indeterminacy. *Child Development, 74,* 1275–1296.

Koslowski, B. (1996). *Theory and evidence: The development of scientific reasoning.* Cambridge, MA: MIT Press/Bradford Books.

Kuhn, D. (2000). Theory of mind, metacognition, and reasoning: A life-span perspective. In P. Mitchell & K. J. Riggs (Eds.), *Children's reasoning and the mind* (pp. 301–326). Hove: Psychology Press.

Kuhn, D. (2001). How do people know? *Psychological Science, 12,* 1–8.

Kuhn, D., & Pearsall, S. (2000). Developmental origins of scientific thinking. *Journal of Cognition and Development, 1,* 113–129.

Kuhn, D., Amsel, E., & O'Loughlin, M. (1988). *The development of scientific thinking skills.* Orlando: Academic Press.

Kuhn, D., Garcia-Mila, M., Zohar, A., Andersen, C. (1995). Strategies of knowledge acquisition. *Society for Research in Child Development Monographs, 60* (4), Serial No. 245

Lagattuta, K. H. (2008). Young children's knowledge about the influence of thoughts on emotion in rule situations. *Developmental Science, 11,* 809–818.

Lagattuta, K. H., & Wellman, H. M. (2001). Thinking about the past: Early knowledge about links between prior experience, thinking, and emotion. *Child Development, 72*, 82–102.

Lagatutta, K. H., Wellman, H. M., & Flavell, J. H. (1997). Preschoolers' understanding of the link between thinking and feeling: cognitive cuing and emotion change. *Child Development, 68*, 1081–1104.

Lagatutta, K. H., Sayfan, L., & Blattman, A. J. (2010). Forgetting common ground: six- to seven-year-olds have an over interpretive theory of mind. *Developmental Psychology, 46*, 1417–1432.

Lillard, A. S. (1998). Wanting it to be: children's understanding of the intentions underlying pretense. *Child Development, 69*, 981–993.

Lovett, S. B., & Pillow, B. H. (1995). The development of the ability to distinguish between comprehension and memory: evidence from strategy-selection tasks. *Journal of Educational Psychology, 87*, 523–536.

Lyon, T. D., & Flavell, J. H. (1993). Young children's understanding of forgetting over time. *Child Development, 64*, 789–800.

Lyon, T. D., & Flavell, J. H. (1994). Young children's understanding of "remember" and "forget.". *Child Development, 65*, 1357–1371.

Masangkay, Z. S., McCluskey, K. A., McIntyre, C. W., Sims-Knight, J., Vaughn, B. E., & Flavell, J. H. (1974). The early development of inferences about the visual percepts of others. *Child Development, 45*, 357–368.

Miller, P. H., & Bigi, L. (1979). The development of children's understanding of attention. *Merrill-Palmer Quarterly, 25*, 235–250.

Miller, S. A., Custer, W. L., & Nassau, G. (2000). Children's understanding of the necessity of logically necessary truths. *Cognitive Development, 15*, 383–403.

Mills, C. M., & Keil, F. C. (2005). The development of cynicism. *Psychological Science, 16*, 385–390.

Moll, H., & Tomasello, M. (2006). Level 1 perspective-taking at 24 months of age. *British Journal of Developmental Psychology, 24*, 603–613.

Morris, A. K. (2000). Development of logical reasoning: children's ability to verbally explain the nature of the distinction between logical and nonlogical forms of argument. *Developmental Psychology, 36*, 741–758.

Moshman, D. (1990). The development of metalogical understanding. In W. F. Overton (Ed.), *Reasoning, necessity, and logic: developmental perspectives* (pp. 205–225). New Jersey: Lawrence Erlbaum Associates.

Moshman, D. (1998). Cognitive development beyond childhood. In W. Damon (Ed.), *Handbook of child psychology: Volume 2: Cognition, perception, and language* (pp. 947–978). New.Jersey: Wiley.

Moshman, D. (2005). *Adolescent psychological development: Rationality, morality, and Identity* (2nd ed.). New Jersey: Lawrence Erlbaum Associates.

Moshman, D., & Franks, B. A. (1986). Development of the concept of inferential validity. *Child Development, 57*, 153–165.

Moynahan, E. D. (1978). Assessment and selection of paired associate strategies: a developmental study. *Journal of Experimental Child Psychology, 26*, 257–266.

Nunner-Winkler, G., & Sodian, B. (1988). Children's understanding of moral emotions. *Child Development, 59*, 1323–1328.

Onishi, K. H., & Baillargeon, R. (2005). Do 15-month-old infants understand false beliefs? *Science, 308*, 255–258.

Parault, S. J., & Schwanenflugel, P. J. (2000). The development of conceptual categories of attention during the elementary school years. *Journal of Experimental Psychology, 75*, 245–262.

Perner, J. (1991). *Understanding the representational mind*. Cambridge, MA: The MIT Press.

Perry, W. G. (1970). *Forms of intellectual and ethical development in the college years*. New York: Holt, Rinehart & Winston.

Piaget, J. (1929). *The child's conception of the world*. London: Routledge and Kegan Paul.

Pierraut-LeBonniec, G. (1980). *The development of modal reasoning: The genesis of necessity and possibility notions*. New York: Academic Press.

Pillow, B. H. (1988). The development of children's beliefs about the mental world. *Merrill-Palmer Quarterly, 34*, 1–32.

Pillow, B. H. (1989a). Early understanding of perception as a source of knowledge. *Journal of Experimental Child Psychology, 47*, 116–129.

Pillow, B. H. (1989b). The development of beliefs about selective attention. *Merrill-Palmer Quarterly, 35*, 421–443.

Pillow, B. H. (1991). Children's understanding of biased social cognition. *Developmental Psychology, 27*, 539–551.

Pillow, B. H. (1995). Two trends in the development of conceptual perspective-taking: an elaboration of the passive-active hypothesis. *International Journal of Behavioral Development, 18*, 649–676.

Pillow, B. H. (1999). Children's understanding of inference and knowledge. *The Journal of Genetic Psychology, 160*, 419–428.

Pillow, B. H. (2002). Children's and adults' evaluation of the certainty of deductive inferences, inductive inferences, and guesses. *Child Development, 73*, 779–792.

Pillow, B.H. & Pearson, R.M. (April, 2011). *Children's and adults' differentiation of controlled and automatic cognitive activities.* Poster presented at the Biennial Meeting of the Society for Research in Child Development, Montreal, Canada

Pillow, B. H., & Henrichon, A. J. (1996). There's more to the picture than meets the eye: young children's difficulty understanding interpretation. *Child Development, 67*, 808–819.

Pillow, B. H., & Lovett, S. B. (1998). "He forgot": Young children's use of cognitive explanations for another person's mistakes. *Merrill-Palmer Quarterly, 44*, 378–403.

Pillow, B. H., & Mash, C. (1999). Young children's understanding of interpretation, expectation, and direct perception as sources of false belief. *British Journal of Developmental Psychology, 17*, 263–276.

Pillow, B. H., & Pearson, R. M. (2009). Children's and adults' evaluation of their own inductive inferences, deductive inferences, and guesses. *Merrill-Palmer Quarterly, 55*, 135–156.

Pillow, B. H., Hill, V., Boyce, A., & Stein, C. (2000). Understanding inference as a source of knowledge: children's ability to evaluate the certainty of deduction, perception, and guessing. *Developmental Psychology, 36*, 169–179.

Pratt, C., & Bryant, P. E. (1990). Young children understand that looking leads to knowing (So long as they are looking into a single barrel). *Child Development, 61*, 973–982.

Roberts, R. J., & Patterson, C. J. (1983). Perspective-taking and referential communication: the question of correspondence reconsidered. *Child Development, 54*, 1005–1014.

Robinson, E. J., & Apperly, I. (1998). Adolescents' and adults' views about the evidential basis for beliefs: relativism and determinism re-examined. *Developmental Science, 1*, 279–289.

Rowley, M., & Robinson, E. J. (2002). Adolescents' judgements about the evidential basis for complex beliefs. *International Journal of Behavioral Development, 26*, 259–268.

Ruffman, T. (1996). Do children understand the mind by means of simulation or theory? Evidence from their understanding of inference. *Mind and Language, 11*, 388–414.

Schraw, G., & Moshman, D. (1995). Metacognitive theories. *Educational Psychology Review, 7*, 351–371.

Schwanenflugel, P. J., Fabricius, W. V., & Alexander, J. (1994). Developing theories of mind: understanding concepts and relations between mental activities. *Child Development, 65*, 1546–1563.

Schwanenflugel, P. J., Fabricius, W. V., & Noyes, C. R. (1996). Developing organization of mental verbs: evidence for the development of a constructivist theory of mind in middle childhood. *Cognitive Development, 11*, 265–294.

Schwanenflugel, P. J., Henderson, R. L., & Fabricius, W. V. (1998). Developing organization of mental verbs and theory of mind in middle childhood: evidence from extensions. *Developmental Psychology, 34*, 512–524.

Selman, R. L. (1980). *The growth of interpersonal understanding.* New York: Academic Press.

Shultz, T. R., & Wells, D. (1985). Judging the intentionality of action-outcomes. *Developmental Psychology, 21*, 83–89.

Sobel, D. M., & Lillard, A. S. (2001). The impact of fantasy and action on young children's understanding of pretence. *British Journal of Developmental Psychology, 19*, 85–98.

Sodian, B. (1988). Children's attributions of knowledge to the listener in a referential communication task. *Child Development, 59*, 378–385.

Sodian, B., & Schneider, W. (1990). Children's understanding of cognitive cuing: How to manipulate cues to fool a competitor. *Child Development, 61*, 697–704.

Sodian, B., & Wimmer, H. (1987). Children's understanding of inference as a source of knowledge. *Child Development, 58*, 424–433.

Sodian, B., Zaitchik, D., & Carey, S. (1991). Young children's differentiation of hypothetical beliefs from evidence. *Child Development, 62*, 753–766.

Taylor, M. (1988). Conceptual perspective taking: children's ability to distinguish what they know from what they see. *Child Development, 59*, 703–711.

Taylor, M., Cartwright, B., & Bowden, T. (1991). Perspective-taking and theory of mind: do children predict interpretive diversity as a function of differences in observer's knowledge? *Child Development, 62*, 1334–1351.

Thoermer, C., & Sodian, B. (2002). Science undergraduates' and graduates' epistemologies of science: the notion of interpretive frameworks. *New Ideas in Psychology, 20*, 263–283.

Varouxaki, A., Freeman, N. H., Peters, D., & Lewis, C. (1999). Inference neglect and ignorance denial. *British Journal of Developmental Psychology, 17*, 483–499.

Wellman, H. M. (1977). Tip of the tongue and feeling of knowing experiences: a developmental study of memory monitoring. *Child Development, 48*, 13–21.

Wellman, H. M. (1990). *The child's theory of mind*. Cambridge, MA: MIT Press.

Wellman, H. M., & Estes, D. (1986). Early understanding of mental entities: a re-examination of childhood realism. *Child Development, 57*, 910–923.

Wellman, H. M., & Johnson, C. N. (1979). Understanding of mental processes: a developmental study of "remember" and "forget.". *Child Development, 50*, 79–88.

Wellman, H. M., Harris, P. L., Banerjee, M., & Sinclair, A. (1995). Early understanding of emotion: evidence from natural language. *Cognition and Emotion, 9*, 117–149.

Wimmer, H., & Perner, J. (1983). Beliefs about beliefs: Representation and constraining function of wrong beliefs in young children's understanding of deception. *Cognition, 13*, 103–128.

Woodward, A. L. (2009). Infants' grasp of others' intentions. *Current Directions in Psychological Science, 18*, 53–57.

Woolley, J. D., & Boerger, E. A. (2002). Development of beliefs about the origins and controllability of dreams. *Developmental Psychology, 38*, 24–41.

Chapter 3
Phenomenological Awareness: Consciousness and the Development of Cognitive Monitoring

Abstract The availability of cues associated with cognitive activity is discussed. Theories of consciousness and metacognition are presented and used to frame consideration of first-person experience as a basis for concepts of cognition. Although conscious access is limited, cues associated with cognitive activity are available to monitoring. However, those cues require interpretation. Introspection, or cognitive monitoring, may inform concepts of cognition, but in turn, knowledge about cognitive functioning may influence the interpretation of cues associated with cognitive activities. The development of cognitive monitoring is discussed, with a focus on studies concerning monitoring of informational content, informational source, feelings of effort and certainty, and emotion. Children's potential use of cognitive monitoring as a source of information for learning about cognitive activities is considered.

A week after finishing kindergarten, my son (age six and one half years) related the following mnemonic experience: "Even though it's after the last day of kindergarten, I can still remember everything about my first day of kindergarten. It feels like I'm seeing the classroom the way it was on the first day." By commenting not only on the content of his memory, but also on the vividness of the experience (i.e., likening it to visual perception), Matthew conveyed some awareness of the phenomenological character of his recall.

Theorizing about the nature and extent of self-awareness has a long history in psychology. In his analysis of the stream of conscious and self-concept, James (1890) distinguished between the self as subject (or I-self) and self as object (or Me-self). The self as subject is our self-awareness and the self as object refers to those aspects of ourselves that we are able to observe and know about. The self as subject includes awareness of internal states, agency, and continuity of the self over time, and self-coherence, while the self as object includes knowledge of physical attributes, social behavior, and psychological qualities. James viewed a process of self-observation, including awareness of internal states, as central to the

B. H. Pillow, *Children's Discovery of the Active Mind*,
SpringerBriefs in Child Development, DOI: 10.1007/978-1-4614-2248-8_3,
© Bradford H. Pillow 2012

construction of a self-concept. Piaget regarded self-awareness as necessary for understanding of other people. According to Piaget's (1929) early theory of egocentrism, young children lack the self-awareness necessary to differentiate between a subjective self and an objective world. Consequently, they take their own experience as reality and cannot conceive of alternative points of view. The emergence of self awareness brings with it recognition of other perspectives. In contrast, Bem's (1972) self-perception theory asserted that individual's know both self and other primarily through third-person observation. Likewise, Nisbett and Wilson (1977) argued that self-reports reflect intuitive psychological theories rather than introspective access, and Wimmer and Hartl (1991) and Gopnik (1993) argued that young children cannot accurately report on their own mental states.

3.1 Theories of Consciousness and Metacognition

Although debate continues concerning the extent of phenomenological awareness and its utility for development (e.g., Carruthers 2009, and accompanying commentary), there is general agreement that cognitive processes are largely unconscious. Thus, conscious access to underlying cognitive processes is strictly limited. Despite such limitations, a number of theorists suggest that when integrated with other sources of information, first-person experience may inform social cognitive development (e.g., Humphrey 1986; Lillard 1999; Moore 2006; Tomasello 1999), and theories of consciousness and theories of metacognition suggest the occurrence of reciprocal influence between phenomenological awareness and conceptual knowledge of cognitive activities (e.g., Flavell 1981; Humphrey 1983, 1986; Mandler 2002).

Mandler (2002) characterizes consciousness as a state of a cognitive structure. Individuals experience the contents of consciousness—thoughts, feelings, images, beliefs, etc. These conscious contents are the outcomes of more complex unconscious processes. Conscious outcomes can be compared and evaluated and then acted upon by unconscious processes. Furthermore, Mandler suggests that the act of examining one's conscious content may alter it. An individual may have a private theory of mental life for which phenomenal experience is a type of data, but such theories are indirect constructions and may not be wholly accurate. Verbally expressing conscious experience also requires transforming it, so that phenomenal experience cannot be directly shared. According to Mandler, the development of consciousness depends upon on individual's interactions with the environment. These interactions determine which cognitive structures become conscious. Consequently, the contents of consciousness may vary across individuals, groups, and cultures.

For Humphrey (1983, 1986), consciousness provides an "inner eye", allowing self-observation. Self-observation facilitates development of a conceptual model of the causal structure of action. Introspective awareness of a self that wills actions motivated by subjective states, such as emotions, sensations, thoughts, and desires, enables individuals to discover links among their overt actions, antecedent conditions, and subjective experiences. The resulting model of one's own causal structure can be extended by analogy for the purpose of understanding the behavior of others. However, Humphrey views introspective access as partial and selective, and, like Mandler, he suggests that conscious experience is not directly reportable. Humphrey also argues that social experiences, such as teasing and initiation rites, create subjective experiences that provide insight into psychological functioning.

The accounts of consciousness proposed by Mandler (2002) and by Humphrey (1983, 1986) imply that phenomenological awareness of cognitive activities is limited and indirect. Conscious experience is limited to outcomes of cognitive processes, but most processes are themselves inaccessible. Although phenomenological awareness informs conceptual knowledge, of cognitive functioning, introspection on cognitive activities requires an interpretation of consciously experienced cues. Introspective knowledge is not perfectly valid, but involves construction. Nevertheless, such knowledge is useful. Arguing that even with distortions introspection provides important information, Nelson and Narens (1990) observed "A system that monitors itself (even imperfectly) may use its own introspections as input..." (p. 128). Moreover, social and cultural experiences influence the development of phenomenological awareness. Phenomenological awareness of cognitive activities provides a limited source of data for building conceptual knowledge, and both a child's conceptual knowledge of mental functioning and social experience may influence the interpretation of phenomenological cues.

Recent models of metacognition view metacognitive judgments, such as the feeling of knowing, or judgments of certainty, as deriving from the interpretation of conscious cues (e.g., Koriat 1998; Lories and Schelstraete 1998; Nelson et al. 1998). Nelson et al. (1998) contend that preexisting concepts or principles are used to interpret subjective feelings. A given cue, such as a feeling of familiarity, may be interpreted in many ways. Support for this position comes from a study by Clore and Parrot (1994). Adults who had been encouraged to attribute hypnotically induced feelings of uncertainty to the hypnotism rated their comprehension of a poem higher than did participants who were given no suggestion concerning the source of their uncertainty. Both Lories and Schelstraete (1998) and Koriat (1998) have suggested that feeling-of-knowing judgments are interpretations of cues associated with retrieval activities rather than products of direct introspective access. The feeling of knowing refers to a person's judgment of his or her ability to recall or recognize information that is not currently accessible. In the Lories and Schelstraete model, when the answer to a question is not retrieved, the amount of ancillary information relevant to the question that is retrieved determines the strength of a person's feeling-of-knowing judgment. In Koriat's accessibility theory, both the amount of information retrieved and the ease of accessing information serve as cues for feeling-of-knowing judgments. As these theories imply, interpretation of conscious cues both informs theories or concepts of mental functioning and is influenced by them.

Children's knowledge of mental states facilitates monitoring of informational content. Detecting a change in content, such as a change in knowledge or belief, suggests a mental event to be explained. Children might explain such changes by appealing to the perception of external events (e.g., "I thought there was candy in the box, but then I opened it and saw pencils."), or by postulating an internal psychological process (e.g., "I knew there were a red marble and a blue marble. I saw the red one in the first box, so I figured out that the marble in the other box was blue."). Monitoring source and effort cues could provide additional evidence for the occurrence of intervening cognitive activity. Thus, children could begin to conceptualize specific patterns of change in mental states. This knowledge of the occurrence of cognitive activities in turn should facilitate the further development of source monitoring. Combined with occurrence knowledge, monitoring of certainty and clarity could provide additional information about the characteristics of cognitive activities. Knowledge of informational input–output patterns, certainty, and effort provides a basis for comparing and contrasting different psychological concepts and experiences, resulting in the development of an organizational model for thinking about cognitive activities. Recognition of the occurrence and effects of cognitive activities, along with children's increasing recognition of the mind as organized entity, may stimulate epistemological reflection by making children increasingly aware of the subjectivity of knowledge and thought. All of these metacognitive interactions may be further informed by children's social environments.

Reciprocal influence between knowledge and phenomenological experience also plays a central role in metacognitive theories. Flavell's (1981) model of metacognitive development posits reciprocal influence between metacognitive experiences and metacognitive knowledge. Children can derive new knowledge about cognitive activities from monitoring their own performance, and, at the same time, children's existing metacognitive beliefs may influence monitoring.

3.2 Phenomenological Awareness of Five Aspects of Cognition

I propose that awareness of five aspects of cognition may contribute to knowledge of cognitive activities: (1) informational content, (2) informational source, (3) feelings of effort or difficulty, (4) feelings of certainty or uncertainty, clarity or confusion, and (5) emotions associated with cognitive activities or cognitive states. Children's ability to monitor content, source, effort, certainty, and emotion is discussed below.

3.2.1 Informational Content

Awareness of informational content includes perceptual experiences, the conscious experience of thoughts, beliefs, knowledge, and imaginings, and judgments of the availability of information in memory. Because these mental contents are the input and output of underlying cognitive activities, they are indirect cues about the occurrence of those activities. For example, a person may be aware of hearing X, seeing Y, and thinking Z. Perceptual experiences X and Y might be the basis for inferring belief Z, or X and Y might cue the retrieval of Z from memory. The occurrence of X, Y, and Z in close temporal contiguity then provides a cue to the occurrence of some underlying activity relating these three conscious states.

Young children have some limited ability to monitor informational content. Three-year-olds have difficulty in reporting past false beliefs, but can accurately report past perceptions, images, and pretenses (Gopnik and Astington 1988; Gopnik and Slaughter 1991). Four- and 5-year-olds generally are accurate at reporting past mental states, including past false beliefs. However, reporting past ignorance may be difficult. Thus, 4-year-olds, and some 5-year-olds, often claim that have known recently learned facts for a long time (Taylor et al. 1994). Reporting an ongoing, or recent, stream of consciousness appears challenging for young children. Before approximately 5- or 6-years of age, children have difficulty reporting aloud the content of their ongoing stream of consciousness, the occurrence of inner speech, or the occurrence of any thoughts at all (Flavell et al. 1995b, 2000, 1997; Kipp and Pope 1997).

Although young children are able to monitor the availability of information in memory, feeling-of-knowing accuracy improves with age and monitoring remains challenging for older children. Thus, with simple materials, 4- and 5-year-olds can make feeling-of-knowing judgments that accurately predict recognition performance (Cultice et al. 1983), but feeling-of-knowing accuracy improves between kindergarten and third-grade (Wellman 1977). Children as young as 6-years also make accurate predictions concerning performance on tests of their memory for recently studied material (Schneider et al. 2000). Monitoring of test performance improves throughout the elementary school years (Pressley and Ghatala 1989). Nevertheless, even older children and adults may have difficulty with spontaneous memory monitoring (Ghatala et al. 1989; Pressley et al. 1987). Among adults such judgments-of-learning (JOL) are more accurate when made following a delay rather than immediately after study (Nelson and Dunlosky 1991; Dunlosky and Nelson 1994). According to Nelson and Dunlosky (1991), the delayed JOL effect occurs because immediate JOLs are influenced by the status of items in short-term memory, but delayed JOLs, made after the items are no longer available to short-term memory, are influenced by the status of items in long-term memory. Consequently, delayed JOLs better predict performance on tests requiring retrieval from long-term memory. Schneider et al. (2000) reported the delayed JOL effect among children aged 6–10 years of age and found accuracy did not change over this age span. This finding indicates that, like adults, children as young as 6-years base their JOLs on items' status in memory at the time judgments are made. Monitoring of test performance improves throughout the elementary school years (Pressley and Ghatala 1989). Nevertheless, even older children and adults may have difficulty with spontaneous memory monitoring. For example, Ghatala et al. (1989) found that after being instructed to read an essay until they had mastered its content, fourth graders often ceased studying before full mastery had been achieved. Pressley et al. (1987) reported that college students had difficulty assessing readiness for a test of textbook material. Memory monitoring, feeling-of-knowing judgments and judgments of learning may be useful for learning about the occurrence of remembering and forgetting, the characteristics of each process, and efficacy of deliberate mnemonic strategies.

Young children sometimes demonstrate awareness of mental activity. Estes (1998) presented children and adults with a task that could be solved by using mental rotation. They were asked to determine whether two monkeys arranged in different spatial orientations were holding up the same arm or different arms. Both 6-year-olds and adults reported using mental rotation, and their reaction times were consistent with doing so (i.e., longer reaction times for problems requiring greater rotation). Most 4-year-olds neither used nor reported mental rotation, but nearly half of 5-year-olds reported mental rotation and appeared to have used it.

Overall, children's ability to report the content of their thoughts appears to improve greatly between 3 and 8 years of age, and continues to improve between 8 years and adulthood. Four- and 5-year-olds have some ability to make feeling-of-knowing judgments, but 5-year-olds have only limited ability to reflect on their own stream of consciousness. By 8 years of age, these abilities improve, but monitoring the availability of information in memory continues to improve and remains difficult even for adults. These age-related improvements in children's introspection suggest that awareness of informational content is more likely to function as a cue to the occurrence of cognitive activities after approximately 7 years of age, but is not entirely absent at earlier ages.

3.2.2 Information Source

Monitoring the source of information could help children learn about the characteristics of specific cognitive activities, the situations in which they occur, and their typical outcomes. Source monitoring is assumed to be an inferential process based on consciously experienced cues. For example, within Johnson's source monitoring model, deliberate, effortful cognitive activities are more likely to leave cues to their occurrence in memory than are automatic, unconscious processes (Johnson et al. 1993; Johnson and Raye 1981). Consequently, internally generated memories (those derived from past thoughts, inferences, imagination, etc.) typically contain more cues about cognitive operations than do perceptually generated memories. Perceptually generated memories contain more perceptual detail and contextual information. Source attributions can be made by evaluating whether the characteristics of a memory are more typical of perceptual events or internally generated events. Source is not a single cue, but rather a judgment based on evaluation of a constellation of cues. This framework implies that developmental changes in children's source monitoring performance may reflect both improvements in children's sensitivity to relevant cues and improvements in children's evaluation of cues.

Young children appear to have some ability to identify the sources of their memories and beliefs, but source monitoring improves with age. In particular, young children sometimes may have difficulty identifying inference as a source of information. O'Neill and Gopnik (1991) reported that 4- and 5-year-olds distinguished among seeing, being told, and touching as sources of knowledge, but 4-year-olds had trouble distinguishing inference from these three perceptual sources. Woolley and Bruell (1996) found that 4- and 5-year-olds distinguished among seeing, being told, imagining, and inferring as sources of belief both immediately after the fact and following a ten-minute delay. In contrast, 3-year-olds correctly indicated whether they had seen the content of a box, been told about it, or imagined it, but typically did not distinguish inference from other sources. During reading comprehension, elementary school children sometimes fail to recognize when knowledge has been inferred rather than presented in the text. For instance, in a study of monitoring during the comprehension of narrative texts, first- through third-grade children often recognized that knowledge of causal relations was inferred rather than presented in the text; however, first- and second-grade children sometimes underestimated the occurrence of causal inferences during comprehension (Beal 1990). Instead, they attributed inferred causal information to the text. Thus, although some awareness of inferences has been reported in early childhood, children's awareness of their own inferences continues to improve during the early elementary school years.

The difficulty of source monitoring tasks depends upon the length of the memory interval, the number of sources of information presented, and the types of discrimination required. Accurate source monitoring by young children is mostly likely to occur with brief memory intervals of a few minutes (Drummey and Newcombe 2002). When source memory is assessed a week after a new fact has been learned, source memory improves between ages 4- and 6-years, but even 6- and 8-year-olds make frequent errors (Drummey and Newcombe 2002). Furthermore, when children receive information about an object from two different sources, rather than from a single source, 3–5-year-olds have more difficulty in remembering the source for a particular belief about the object (Whitcombe and Robinson 2000). Memories for similar sources are generally more difficult to discriminate from each other than are memories for dissimilar sources (Johnson et al. 1993; Roberts 2002). Six-year-olds are better at discriminating internally generated memories from externally generated memories (e.g., words the child has said vs. words the child has heard someone else say) compared to discriminating between two types of internally generated memories (e.g., words the child has said vs. words the child has imagined saying), but 9-year-olds and adults perform well on both types of discrimination (Foley et al. 1983). Likewise, 4- and 5-year-olds distinguish memories for actions they have performed from actions they have imagined or pretended, but often confuse memories for imagined and pretended actions (Welch-Ross 1995).

Vividness and contextual detail also provide cues regarding a memory's reliability. According to Brainerd and Reyna's (2004) fuzzy-trace theory, retrieval of verbatim traces is accompanied by vivid, realistic recollective phenomenology, whereas retrieval of gist traces typically is associated with the experience of vague familiarity. When verbatim traces are retrieved, as is likely for true memories of recent events, vivid recollective phenomenology is experienced. In contrast, retrieval of false memories that are consistent with the gist of events is likely to be accompanied by familiarity phenomenology. Adults use this phenomenological difference to evaluate the reliability of memories (e.g., Dodson and Schacter 2002). Between middle childhood and adolescence there is an increase in children's experience of vivid retrieval phenomenology and use of it to evaluate the truth of their recollections (e.g., Brainerd and Reyna 2004; Brainerd et al. 1998).

Source monitoring involves detecting relevant cues, discriminating among them, and inferring the source of information. Although young children demonstrate some source monitoring ability, performance becomes more accurate with increased age as children become more sensitive to phenomenological cues, discriminate more precisely, and better evaluate their meaning. In order to attribute a memory to particular cognitive activity, such as inference, children would have to some initial concept of that activity. However, improved source monitoring during the elementary school years could help children to refine their knowledge of the characteristics of specific cognitive activities, the situations in which they occur, and their typical outcomes.

3.2.3 Feelings of Effort or Difficulty

Feelings of effort or difficulty are potential cues concerning engagement in goal-directed cognitive activity or progress toward cognitive goals. Therefore, feelings of effort or difficulty indicate the occurrence of cognitive activity. Moreover, these cues may provide a basis for inferences concerning the controllability of cognitive processes. Although the relation between feelings of effort or difficulty and controllability is not perfect (e.g., one may sometimes execute a deliberate process with relatively little effort), it may be sufficient to be informative about the distinction between controlled and automatic processes.

Feelings of mental effort may accompany deliberate or strategic cognitive activities, especially when an individual vigilantly monitors performance and engages in sustained or repeated attempts to achieve an outcome. For example, a person may try to recall a name, try to memorize a passage of text or rehearse a phone number, try to maintain a focus of attention, or try to understand a complex and subtle theory. The conscious impression of effort experienced during such attempts may provide a cue to the occurrence of cognitive processing. Although 5-year-olds understand that effort influences cognitive performance (Kun 1977; Wellman et al. 1981), second-grade children sometimes do not estimate relative effort accurately (Nicholls and Miller 1984).

Feelings of difficulty are related to, but not identical to, feelings of effort. Because successful completion of difficult tasks requires effort, feelings of difficulty and effort may occur together; however, one might sense the difficulty of a task and opt not to expend the effort necessary to complete it. When studying for an associative memory task, first- and third-grade children devoted more study time to the names of unfamiliar hard items compared to easy items (Kobasigawa and Metcalf-Haggert 1993). Differential allocation of study time can be taken as an index of children's monitoring of the difficulty of the material and their progress at learning it (Kobasigawa and Metcalf-Haggert 1993). In addition, first-grade children can independently monitor the difficulty of achieving different cognitive goals, such as memorization and comprehension (Lovett and Pillow 1996). Older children are sensitive to changes in feelings of difficulty during problem solving. In a study of mathematical problem solving by Efklides et al. (1999), adolescents ages 13–15 rated feeling of difficulty before attempting problems, while planning their solution, and after producing a solution, and also gave an overall difficulty rating. Feelings of difficulty increased from earlier to later phases of problem solving.

During the elementary school years and adolescence feelings of effort or difficulty are available as a potential source of information about cognitive activities. Detection of effort or difficulty could help children to distinguish between deliberate cognitive activities and automatic processes. A conceptual basis for this distinction appears to develop during middle childhood as children become aware of an ongoing stream of consciousness (Flavell et al. 1993, 1995a, b, 1998), and in adulthood an effortful versus automatic dimension underlies the organization of concepts of attentional activities (Parault and Schwanenflugel 2000). Coordinating of monitoring informational content with monitoring of effort or difficulty, may facilitate children's recognition that cognitive processing often occurs in the absence of effort or difficulty cues, and this recognition may be important for learning about automatic processes.

3.2.4 Feelings of Certainty or Uncertainty

Feelings of certainty, uncertainty, clarity or confusion, serve as cues about the progress of cognitive activities. Potentially, these metacognitive experiences could help children identify circumstances and strategies that facilitate or hinder comprehension, reasoning, or problem solving. Uncertainty may signal inadequacies or inconsistencies in informational input, as in the case of ambiguous verbal messages or contradictory instructions. Alternatively, uncertainty and confusion may indicate errors in children's thinking.

Children in kindergarten through second-grade often fail to detect, interpret, or utilize uncertainty cues (Flavell et al. 1985, 1981; Harris et al. 1981; Markman 1981). Nevertheless, young children sometimes do demonstrate awareness of uncertainty. For example, 4–6-year-old children rated themselves as more certain about the meaning of an unambiguous message than about the meaning of an ambiguous message (Robinson and Whittaker 1985). When directed to attend to the ease with which a response comes to mind, children as young as 3-years of age demonstrate the ability to monitor their own sense of uncertainty by reporting greater confidence for accurate answers than for inaccurate answers (Lyons and Ghetti 2011). Older children increasingly recognize feelings of certainty as a cue to differences among cognitive activities, such as deduction, induction, and guessing (Galotti et al. 1997; Pillow 2002) or comprehension and memorization (Lovett and Pillow 1996). In general, young children often appear insensitive to the occurrence or significance of uncertainty, but they are not wholly unable to detect it, and monitoring of certainty or uncertainty improves during early elementary school years.

3.2.5 Emotions Associated with Cognitive States or Activities

Because happiness, sadness, anger, fear, surprise, and other emotions are subjective states, true conceptual understanding of emotional functioning requires appreciation of the subjective experience of affective states. To have a complete concept of happiness, sadness, or anger, one must have some sense of what it feels like to experience those emotions. Thus, awareness of one's own emotions presumably is necessary for the development of mature knowledge of emotion. Monitoring ongoing emotions, as well as reflecting on past emotional experiences, could provide information not only about the nature of emotion, but also about psychological functioning more generally. Emotion monitoring could include: (1) detecting one's current emotional state, (2) detecting associations between emotional states and overt events, associations between emotional states and thoughts, or associations among emotions, overt events, and thoughts, and (3) detecting causal connections between emotions and overt events or thoughts. Detection of associations or causal connections could be useful for learning about cognitive activities. In general, emotions may increase the salience of associated mental states or cognitive processes. Potentially, emotion monitoring may then facilitate cognitive monitoring. By highlighting changes in mental states, emotions might facilitate awareness of cognitive activities underlying changes in cognitive states. For example, confronted by circumstances at odds with one's expectations, a person may feel surprise, disappointment, or perhaps elation, accompanying a sudden shift in beliefs about the world. Such affective experiences may heighten awareness of mental events and motivate efforts to explain them. More specifically, monitoring emotion may contribute to learning about influence of emotion on cognition and the cognitive mediation of emotional responses.

Most research on children's knowledge of emotion has examined age-related changes in children's understanding of emotional functioning, rather than children's monitoring of their own emotional experiences. Thus, a great deal of research has investigated children's ability to predict or explain another person's emotional response in a given set of circumstances. On the basis of such research, Harris (1995) argues that young children lack awareness of their own emotions. As Harris notes, by about 3-years of age children appear to regard emotions as internal states that may vary across individuals, children reason about the causes of emotions (e.g., John is mad because Mary broke his favorite toy), and children also recognize the targets of emotions (e.g., John is mad at Mary). At the same time, Harris claims that there are cognitive limitations on children's awareness of emotion. In support of this view, he cites young children's difficulty understanding mixed emotions, and young children's difficulty predicting emotions on the basis of false beliefs.

When asked to describe situations that would elicit both positive and negative emotions at the same time, 4- and 5-year-olds denied the possibility of feeling two emotions at once (Harter 1983). Children did not provide clear examples of situations that produce simultaneous conflicting emotions until 10 or 11 years of age. Likewise, when given examples of situations characterized by conflicting elements and asked which of a set of four emotions they would feel in each situation, 6-year-olds rarely suggested that they would feel two emotions with opposite valences simultaneously (Harris 1983). Ten-year-olds were much more likely than 6-year-olds to predict conflicting emotions, but still did so for less than half of the stories on average. To account for these results, Harris (1995) distinguishes between two appraisal systems. The first is an automatic system that produces the child's emotional response to a situation. This automatic system exhaustively scans for emotionally significant cues. Thus, it detects and responds to a wide variety of environmental features, including both positive and negative aspects of another person's behavior, etc. The second appraisal system is a self-conscious system that children use to identify their own emotions. This self-conscious system is less exhaustive. Once this system finds emotionally significant elements in the environment, children cease scanning and make their appraisal of the situation. Consequently, children are likely to characterize events in terms of a single emotion at a time. With increased age, children gradually become more likely to engage in exhaustive appraisal with the self-conscious system, facilitating knowledge of mixed emotions. As further evidence, Peng et al. (1992) reported that encouraging more exhaustive appraisal of situations with emotionally conflicting cues resulted in increased judgments of mixed emotions by 6- and 7-year-olds, but not by 4- and 5-year-olds.

As discussed earlier, when predicting emotional reactions, 6-year-olds consider a person's beliefs and desires, as well as objective reality. In contrast, 4-year-olds recognize the importance of desires and reality, but typically fail to account for a person's beliefs (Harris et al. 1989). Harris (1995) suggests that young children's difficulty in understanding the significance of beliefs for another person's emotion reflects limitations on children's awareness of their own emotional experience. Young children often have difficulty reporting on their own past false belief after they have discovered the truth (Astington and Gopnik 1998; Wimmer and Hartl 1991). Therefore, Harris speculates that young children should also have difficulty in reconstructing past emotions that were based on false beliefs that the children no longer hold. According to Harris, young children may be able to report current emotions stemming from currently held false beliefs, but once children's belief has changed and the emotion has passed, children should be unable to recall or reconstruct their prior feelings.

Although Harris's proposal that children lack emotional awareness is plausible and intriguing, the development of children's ability to monitor their own emotions has not been directly assessed in studies of children's reasoning about emotion. Understanding of emotion could be informed by both first-person awareness of one's own emotion and third-person observation of others' emotional expressions. Therefore, errors in emotional understanding are not necessarily attributable solely to a lack of first-person awareness. Young children might have some ability to monitor ongoing emotions, but still be limited in their ability to learn about emotional functioning from monitoring experiences. As with other types of monitoring, different levels of emotional awareness might emerge in the course of development and occur on different occasions. A brief, fleeting awareness might not be sufficient for learning about relations between emotions and thoughts or relations between emotions and situations. Longer duration and more detailed awareness could allow for reflection and analysis. The ability to retain information about emotional experiences and associated events for a few moments after they have occurred, or to recall such experiences at later times, might facilitate identification of emotions, their causes and targets, and other contextual details. Mature individuals might also sometimes monitor emotions deliberately and purposively analyze their experience. Children's ability to monitor and learn from first-person emotional experiences remains to be investigated. However, to the extent that emotional understanding derives from first-person experience, young children's knowledge of emotional cuing (Lagattuta and Wellman 2001) would seem to indicate some early form of emotional awareness.

3.3 Summary

Although introspective access to cognitive states and processes appears to be strictly limited, some theories of consciousness and metacognition suggest that as adults we may consciously experience cues related to occurrence of cognitive processes. Introspection, then, may involve using past experience and concepts to intepret consciously experienced cues. Developmental research indicates that children detect some metacognitive cues at an early age, but that cognitive monitoring continues to improve into adulthood. As monitoring develops, children's phenomenological awareness of cues related to cognitive activities could provide at least a limited source of data for building conceptual knowledge about cognition. At the same time, children's growing conceptual understanding of cognition might enhance their attention to and interpretation of metacognitive cues.

References

Astington, J. W., & Gopnik, A. (1998). Children's understanding of representational change and its relation to the understanding of false belief and the appearance-reality distinction. *Child Development, 59*, 26–37.

Beal, C. R. (1990). Development of knowledge about the role of inference in text comprehension. *Child Development, 61*, 1011–1023.

Bem, D. J. (1972). Self-perception theory. In L. Berkowitz (Ed.), *Advances in experimental social psychology* (Vol. 6, pp. 1–62). New York: Academic.

Brainerd, C. J., & Reyna, V. F. (2004). Fuzzy-trace theory and memory development. *Developmental Review, 24*, 396–439.

Brainerd, C. J., Stein, L., & Reyna, V. F. (1998). On the development of conscious and unconscious memory. *Developmental Psychology, 34*, 342–357.

Carruthers, P. (2009). How we know our own minds: the relationship between mindreading and metacognition. *Behavioral and Brain Sciences, 32*, 121–182.

Clore, G. L., & Parrot, W. G. (1994). Cognitive feelings and metacognitive judgments. *European Journal of Social Psychology, 24*, 101–115.

Cultice, J. C., Somerville, S. C., & Wellman, H. M. (1983). Preschoolers' memory monitoring: feeling of knowing judgments. *Child Development, 54*, 1480–1486.

Dodson, C. S., & Schacter, D. L. (2002). When false recognition meets metacognition: the distinctiveness heuristic. *Journal of Memory and Language, 46*, 782–803.

Drummey, A. B., & Newcombe, N. S. (2002). Developmental changes in source memory. *Developmental Science, 5*, 502–513.

Dunlosky, J., & Nelson, T. O. (1994). Does the sensitivity of judgments of learning (JOLs) to the effects of various study activities depend on when the JOLs occur? *Journal of Memory and Language, 33*, 545–565.

Efklides, A., Samara, A., & Petropolou, M. (1999). Feeling of difficulty: an aspect of monitoring that influences control. *European Journal of Psychology of Education, 14*, 461–476.

Estes, D. (1998). Young children's awareness of their mental activity: the case of mental rotation. *Child Development, 69*, 1345–1360.

Flavell, J. H. (1981). Cognitive monitoring. In W. P. Dickson (Ed.), *Children's oral communication skills* (pp. 35–60). New York: Academic.

Flavell, J. H., Speer, J. R., Green, F. L., & August, D. L. (1981). The development of comprehension monitoring and knowledge about communication. *Monographs of the Society for Research in Child Development, 46*, 5. Serial No. 192.

Flavell, J. H., Green, F. L., & Flavell, E. R. (1985). The road not taken: Understanding the implications of initial uncertainty in evaluating spatial directions. *Developmental Psychology, 21*, 207–216.

Flavell, J. H., Green, F. L., & Flavell, E. R. (1993). Children's understanding of the stream of consciousness. *Child Development, 64*, 387–398.

Flavell, J. H., Green, F. L., & Flavell, E. R. (1995a). The development of children's knowledge about attentional focus. *Developmental Psychology, 31*, 706–712.

Flavell, J. H., Green, F. L., & Flavell, E. R. (1995b). Young children's knowledge about thinking. *Monographs of the Society for Research in Child Development, 60*, 1. Serial No. 243.

Flavell, J. H., Green, F. L., Flavell, E. R., & Grossman, J. B. (1997). The development of children's knowledge about inner speech. *Child Development, 68*, 39–47.

Flavell, J. H., Green, F. L., & Flavell, E. R. (1998). The mind has a mind of its own: developing knowledge about mental uncontrollability. *Cognitive Development, 13*, 127–138.

Flavell, J. H., Green, F. L., & Flavell, E. R. (2000). Development of children's awareness of their own thoughts. *Journal of Cognition and Development, 1*, 97–112.

Foley, M. A., Johnson, M. K., & Raye, C. L. (1983). Age-related changes in confusion between memories for thoughts and memories for speech. *Child Development, 54*, 51–60.

Galotti, K. M., Komatsu, L. K., & Voelz, S. (1997). Children's differential performance on deductive and inductive syllogisms. *Developmental Psychology, 33*, 70–78.

Ghatala, E. S., Levin, J. R., Foorman, B. R., & Pressley, M. (1989). Improving children's regulation of their reading PREP time. *Contemporary Educational Psychology, 14*, 49–66.

Gopnik, A. (1993). How we know our minds: the illusion of first-person knowledge of intentionality. *Behavioral and Brain Sciences, 16*, 1–14.

Gopnik, A., & Astington, J. W. (1988). Children's understanding of representational change and its relation to the understanding of false belief and the appearance-reality distinction. *Child Development, 59*, 26–37.

Gopnik, A., & Slaughter, V. (1991). Young children's understanding of changes in their mental states. *Child Development, 62,* 98–110.

Harris, P. L. (1983). Children's understanding of the link between situation and emotion. *Journal of Experimental Child Psychology, 36,* 490–509.

Harris, P. L. (1995). Children's awareness and lack of awareness of mind and emotion. In D. Cicchetti & S. L. Toth (Eds.), *Emotion, cognition, and representation* (pp. 35–57). New York: University of Rochester Press.

Harris, P. L., Kruithof, A., Terwogt, M. M., & Visser, T. (1981). Children's detection and awareness of textual anomaly. *Journal of Experimental Child Psychology, 31,* 212–230.

Harris, P. L., Johnson, C. N., Hutton, D., Andrews, G., & Cooke, T. (1989). Young children's theory of mind and emotion. *Cognition and Emotion, 3,* 379–400.

Harter, S. (1983). Children's understanding of multiple emotions: A cognitive-developmental approach. In W. F. Overton (Ed.), *The relationship between social and cognitive development* (pp. 147–194). New Jersey: Lawrence Erlbaum Associates.

Humphrey, N. (1983). *Consciousness regained: Chapters in the development of mind.* Oxford: Oxford University Press.

Humphrey, N. (1986). *The inner eye.* London: Faber and Faber.

James, W. (1890). *The principles of psychology.* Cambridge: Harvard University Press. (1890/ 1983).

Johnson, M. K., & Raye, C. L. (1981). Reality monitoring. *Psychological Review, 88,* 67–85.

Johnson, M. K., Hashtroudi, S., & Lindsay, D. S. (1993). Source monitoring. *Psychological Bulletin, 114,* 3–28.

Kipp, K., & Pope, S. (1997). The development of cognitive inhibition in streams-of-consciousness and directed speech. *Cognitive Development, 12,* 239–260.

Kobasigawa, A., & Metcalf-Haggert, A. (1993). Spontaneous allocation of study time by first- and third-grade children in a simple memory task. *Journal of Genetic Psychology, 154,* 223–235.

Koriat, A. (1998). Illusions of knowing: The link between knowledge and metaknowledge. In V. Y. Yzerbyt, G. Lories, & B. Dardenne (Eds.), *Metacognition: Cognitive and social dimensions* (pp. 16–34). London: Sage Publications.

Kun, A. (1977). Development of the magnitude-covariation and compensation schemata in ability and effort attributions of performance. *Child Development, 48,* 862–873.

Lagattuta, K. H., & Wellman, H. M. (2001). Thinking about the past: Early knowledge about links between prior experience, thinking, and emotion. *Child Development, 72,* 82–102.

Lillard, A. (1999). Developing a cultural theory of mind: the CIAO approach. *Current Directions in Psychological Science, 8,* 57–61.

Lories, G., & Schelstraete, M. (1998). The feeling-of-knowing as a judgment. In V. Y. Yzerbyt, G. Lories, & B. Dardenne (Eds.), *Metacognition: Cognitive and social dimensions* (pp. 53–68). London: Sage Publications.

Lovett, S. B., & Pillow, B. H. (1996). The development of the ability to distinguish between comprehension and memory: evidence from goal-state evaluation tasks. *Journal of Educational Psychology, 88,* 546–562.

Lyons, K., Ghetti, S. (2011). The development of uncertainty monitoring in early childhood. *Child Development.*

Mandler, G. (2002). *Consciousness recovered: Psychological functions and origins of conscious.* Amsterdam: John Benjamins Publishing Company.

Markman, E. M. (1981). Comprehension monitoring. In W. P. Dickson (Ed.), *Children's oral communication skills* (pp. 61–84). New York: Academic.

Moore, C. (2006). *The development of commonsense psychology.* New Jersey: Lawrence Erlbaum Associates.

Nelson, T. O., & Dunlosky, J. (1991). When people's judgments of learning (JOLs) are extremely accurate at predicting subsequent recall: the "delayed-JOL effect". *Psychological Science, 2,* 267–270.

Nelson, T. O., & Narens, L. (1990). Metamemory: A theoretical framework and some new findings. In G. Bower (Ed.), *The psychology of learning and motivation* (pp. 125–173). San Diego: Academic.

Nelson, T. O., Kruglanski, A. W., & Jost, J. T. (1998). Knowing thyself and others: Progress in metacognitive social psychology. In V. Y. Yzerbyt, G. Lories, & D. Benoit (Eds.), *Metacognition: Cognitive and social dimensions* (pp. 69–89). London: Sage Publications.

Nicholls, J. G., & Miller, A. T. (1984). Reasoning about the ability of self and others: a developmental study. *Child Development, 55*, 1990–1999.

Nisbett, R. E., & Wilson, T. D. (1977). Telling more than we can know: verbal reports on mental processes. *Psychological Review, 84*, 231–259.

O'Neill, D. K., & Gopnik, A. (1991). Young children's ability to identify the sources of their beliefs. *Developmental Psychology, 27*, 390–397.

Parault, S. J., & Schwanenflugel, P. J. (2000). The development of conceptual categories of attention during the elementary school years. *Journal of Experimental Psychology, 75*, 245–262.

Peng, M., Johnson, C. N., Pollock, J., Glasspool, R., & Harris, P. L. (1992). Training young children to acknowledge mixed emotions. *Cognition and Emotion, 6*, 387–401.

Piaget, J. (1929). *The child's conception of the world*. London: Routledge and Kegan Paul.

Pillow, B. H. (2002). Children's and adults' evaluation of the certainty of deductive inferences, inductive inferences, and guesses. *Child Development, 73*, 779–792.

Pressley, M., & Ghatala, E. S. (1989). Metacognitive benefits of taking a test for children and young adolescents. *Journal of Experimental Child Psychology, 47*, 430–450.

Pressley, M., Snyder, B. L., Levin, J. R., Murray, H. G., & Ghatala, E. S. (1987). Perceived readiness for examination performance (PREP) produced by initial reading of text and text containing adjunct questions. *Reading Research Quarterly, 22*, 219–236.

Roberts, K. P. (2002). Children's ability to distinguish between memories from multiple sources: implications for the quality and accuracy of eyewitness statements. *Developmental Review, 22*, 403–435.

Robinson, E. J., & Whittaker, S. J. (1985). Children's responses to ambiguous messages and their understanding of ambiguity. *Developmental Psychology, 21*, 446–454.

Schneider, W., Vise, M., Lockl, K., & Nelson, T. O. (2000). Developmental trends in children's memory monitoring: evidence from a judgment-of-learning task. *Cognitive Development, 15*, 115–134.

Taylor, M., Esbensen, B. M., & Bennett, R. T. (1994). Children's understanding of knowledge acquisition: the tendency for children to report that they have always known what they have just learned. *Child Development, 65*, 1581–1604.

Tomasello, M. (1999). Having intentions, understanding intentions, and understanding communicative intentions. In P. D. Zelazo, J. W. Astington, & D. R. Olson (Eds.), *Developing theories of intention: Social understanding and self-control* (pp. 63–76). Nwe Jersey: Lawrence Erlbaum Associates.

Welch-Ross, M. K. (1995). Developmental changes in preschoolers' ability to distinguish memories of performed, pretended, and imagined actions. *Cognitive Development, 10*, 421–441.

Wellman, H. M. (1977). Tip of the tongue and feeling of knowing experiences: A developmental study of memory monitoring. *Child Development, 48*, 13–21.

Wellman, H. M., Collins, J., & Glieberman, J. (1981). Understanding the combination of memory variables: developing conceptions of memory limitations. *Child Development, 52*, 1313–1317.

Whitcombe, E. L., & Robinson, E. J. (2000). Children's decisions about what to believe and their ability to report the source of their belief. *Cognitive Development, 15*, 329–346.

Wimmer, H., & Hartl, M. (1991). Against the Cartesian view on mind: young children's difficulty with own false beliefs. *British Journal of Developmental Psychology, 9*, 125–138.

Woolley, J. D., & Bruell, M. J. (1996). Young children's awareness of the origins of their mental representations. *Developmental Psychology, 32*, 335–346.

Chapter 4
Social Experience as a Source
of Information About Mental Events

Abstract Social influences on children's metacognitive knowledge are considered. Learning about cognitive activities takes place in social contexts, and knowledge of cognitive activities often is used for social purposes and is manifested through social acts. Socio-cultural theories emphasize intersubjectivity during social interaction as a mechanism of cognitive development. In this chapter, learning about the mind via observation, conversation, and formal education are discussed. Although there have been few studies relevant to social influences on children's understanding of cognitive activities, many studies have examined social influences on young children's understanding of belief and emotion. This literature is summarized briefly. Implications for social influences on children's understanding of cognition are considered, and the possibility of cultural differences in the development of children's understanding of cognitive activities is discussed

Pay attention to what you're doing. You need to be careful!

Like other parents of young children, I have uttered sentences such as those above more times than I can remember. Parents, teachers, and other adults commonly admonish children to pay attention, listen, remember, or think. Although I have discerned little evidence for the efficacy of such efforts in my own parental experience to date, the research literature offers some hope that comments on mental states and conversations about psychological events facilitate children's learning about the mind.

4.1 Learning in Social Context: Theoretical Perspectives

Learning about cognitive activities takes place in social contexts, and knowledge of cognitive activities often is used for social purposes and is manifested through social acts. Social processes have been a central theme in recent theorizing about

B. H. Pillow, *Children's Discovery of the Active Mind,*
SpringerBriefs in Child Development, DOI: 10.1007/978-1-4614-2248-8_4,
© Bradford H. Pillow 2012

social cognitive development. Focusing on infancy and early childhood, Moore (2006) describes how the coordination of social acts enables the integration of a child's first-person experiences with third-person observation of an adult's actions. According to Moore, this integration facilitates recognition of the equivalence of self and other as intentional agents with subjective experiences, and this recognition provides the basis for the development of further social understanding. In early childhood, language can be used to discuss psychological experiences, and thus furthers children's learning about differences in perspective. Building on Chapman's (1991) view of an epistemic triangle, Carpendale and Lewis (2004) likewise argue that children construct social understanding via participation in social interactions. In a model integrating individual and cultural processes, Lillard (1999) argues that understanding of the mind depends upon culture, introspection, and analogy between self and other. Children notice their own mental states, draw analogies between their actions and experiences and those of others, and learn the prevalent ways of describing behavior in their culture. From all of these perspectives, social processes are integral to the development of social understanding.

Socio-cultural theories emphasize intersubjectivity during social interaction as a mechanism of cognitive development (Rogoff 1990; Tomasello 1999). Tomasello (1999) proposes that discourse confronts children with differing perspectives in three ways. First, during disagreements conversational partners may explicitly express contrasting knowledge or perspectives. Second, a listener may misunderstand a speaker and ask for clarification. Such misunderstandings signal a difference in perspective. Third, didactic interactions may include meta discouse. That is, after a child expresses a view, another person may comment explicitly on the child's view. By stimulating children to examine their own thinking from another person's perspective, such exchanges promote awareness of alternative perspectives and reflection on the child's own mental life. Similarly, Harris et al. (2005) argue that conversation influences children's understanding of mental states by highlighting differences in perspective.

Intersubjectivity also may occur in the course of joint problem solving (Rogoff 1990). As a child and adult jointly construct a shared understanding of a problem and of each others' perspectives, the child may experience new insights into psychological functioning. More generally, children's efforts to explain social experiences and observations may contribute to social cognitive development. As they try to make sense of their social experiences, children's efforts to explain the actions, statements, or thoughts of either self or other may lead to thoughts about psychological functioning. By motivating children's mentalistic explanations, social events may contribute to learning about cognitive activities. In addition, experience with formal education may stimulate children to reflect on their own reasoning, as well as that of others.

Social experience may facilitate the development of conceptual knowledge about cognition by fostering the occurrence of introspection, intersubjectivity, and explanation. Below, empirical research concerning the influence of observation and social interaction on children's knowledge of mental states is reviewed, and the implications of this research for the development of children's conceptual understanding of cognition are considered. Then research on the relation between formal education and epistemological development is discussed.

4.2 Observation

Even in the absence of direct interaction, children's observation of social events, and attempts to explain them, could stimulate insight into cognitive functioning. Children begin learning both from and about the actions of others during infancy. During the first two months of life infants imitate adults' facial and manual gestures (Meltzoff and Moore 1997), and during the first year infants also detect patterns in adults' behavior and form expectations about typical actions and reactions (e.g., Trevarthan and Aitken 2001). For observation to yield insights regarding cognitive activities, children would have to go beyond noticing typical patterns of overt behavior and deviations from them. Children would need to infer mental states and activities underlying observed actions. According to the naive theory approach to children's understanding of mind, children postulate psychological constructs to explain the behavior of both self and others (e.g., Gopnik 1993; Gopnik and Wellman 1992). The resulting theory allows children to make predictions about people's actions and to interpret actions, but is susceptible to change in the face of contradictory evidence. Observing the overt actions of others provides one type of evidence motivating the construction and revision of children's theories. Children also may observe and explain their own actions (Bem 1972; Gopnik 1993).

Young children describe observed behavior in mentalistic terms and also attribute others' actions to internal causes, particularly beliefs and desires (Lillard and Flavell 1990; Miller and Aloise 1989; Wellman 1990). During middle childhood, explanations also include cognitive activities such as forgetting or attending selectively (Pillow and Lovett 1998). Thus, when observing others' behavior, children often think of psychological processes underlying the observed behavior. Observation may stimulate thoughts about cognitive activities. However, the fact that children use psychological constructs to explain observed actions does not necessarily imply that children learn about psychological activities through observation. Two studies provide more direct evidence that children benefit from observing another person's performance.

McGivern et al. (1990) showed second-grade, seventh-grade, and college students a videotape of a model using either verbal repetition or sentence elaboration to learn a list of paired-associate nouns. Students also observed the model's performance on a cued recall test. Both seventh-grade and college students learned about the differential effectiveness of the two memory strategies, but second-grade students did not. Thus, older children were able to acquire strategy knowledge by monitoring another person's performance. This finding suggests that for older children observation may provide information about the occurrence of cognitive activities, especially when cognitive activity is manifested in overt action.

Pillow et al. (2002) investigated 4- and 5-year-old children's understanding that prior experience could bias another observer's interpretation of an ambiguous picture. After being pretested on their ability to recognize that a puppet might misinterpret a drawing after viewing only a small ambiguous region, children participated in training that involved either explaining their own misinterpretation of ambiguous drawings or observing and explaining puppets' misinterpretations of drawings. For self-training children viewed sequences of three drawings (e.g., two sharks followed by a house). Before seeing the full drawing, they viewed a small ambiguous portion (e.g., a triangle corresponding to either the shark's fin or the roof of the house). While viewing the ambiguous part of the third drawing, children were asked (a) what they thought it was, (b) why, and (c) what pictures they had seen before. For other training, children observed a puppet being shown sequences of drawings. While looking at the ambiguous part of the third drawing the puppet stated a misinterpretation of it (e.g., saying "I think it's a shark!" while viewing the roof of the house). Then children were asked (a) to explain the puppet's interpretation, and (b) what pictures the puppet had seen before. Following either type of training, children were more likely to predict a puppet's misinterpretation of ambiguous drawings. Children in a no-training control group did not improve from pre- to post-test. These results are consistent with the possibility that observing overt actions can facilitate understanding of the occurrence of cognitive activities, such as constructive interpretation of visual information.

Observation often may occur during social interactions that include reciprocal influence and possibly explicit or implicit communication of thoughts and feelings. For example, during joint problem solving a child observes an adult's actions, the adult's reactions to the changing problem situation, and the adult's responses to the child's own actions. Such observations provide information concerning the adult's thoughts, and may be accompanied by discussion of the problem, the adult's thoughts, and the child's thoughts.

4.3 Social Interaction

Social interaction encompasses a wide array of experiences. Social interactions include dyadic and group interactions, exchanges between strangers or acquaintances, friends, or relatives, equals or unequals. These exchanges may be scripted or spontaneous, and they may be characterized by collaboration, cooperation, competition, or conflict. Participants may engage in verbal and non-verbal communication, and processes of observation, modeling, reinforcement, perspective-taking, and causal attribution. During an interaction participants influence each others' mental states and actions in both deliberate and unintended ways, though participants may or may not recognize each others' influence. Furthermore, participants bring with them varying levels of metacognitive and social cognitive understanding, and participants may experience metacognitive or social cognitive insights during or following an exchange.

A substantial body of research has examined how social factors, such as family structure, parenting style, linguistic experience, and conversations about mental states are related to young children's understanding of mental states such as belief, desire, and emotion. Because these studies have not examined children's understanding of cognitive activities, they do not directly address the relation between social interaction and the development of conceptual knowledge about cognitive activities. Nevertheless, consideration of the social context in which young children's mental state understanding develops may provide insights that can inform theory and research about later social cognitive development. Therefore, some key findings from this research will be summarized below.

4.3.1 Family Structure

Evidence for associations between family structure and children's understanding of belief is mixed. Three studies have found that having siblings is related to better performance on measures of false belief understanding (Jenkins and Astington 1996; Perner et al. 1994; Ruffman et al. 1998), but others have not found this correlation (Carlson and Moses 2001; Cutting and Dunn 1999; Dunn et al. 1991b; Pears and Moses 2003). In addition, Lewis et al. (1996) found that 3- and 4-year-olds' false belief understanding was related to the number of adult relatives in their household, the number of adults the child interacted with daily, the number of older siblings, and the number of older children the child interacted with daily. Although the connection between family structure and mental state understanding remains to be clarified, the associations reported in some studies raise questions about how patterns of family interaction might be related to social cognitive development.

4.3.2 Parenting Style

Studies of parenting style indicate that social interactions within the family are related to young children's understanding of mental states. Variations in parenting style are related to individual differences in children's behavior and psychological functioning, including differences in social understanding. Secure attachment is related to children's understanding of emotion and false belief (Laible and Thompson 1998; Meins et al. 1998). Maternal responses to children's transgressions also are related to children's understanding of emotion, perception, and belief (Pears and Moses 2003; Ruffman et al. 1999). These findings suggest two pathways for investigation of the relation between parenting style and social understanding during middle and late childhood: (a) parenting style, or the quality of the parent–child relationship, during early childhood could be related to later advances in social cognition, or (b) parental behavior during middle or later childhood could be related to social understanding at those ages.

4.3.3 Language and Conversation

Our mental states are, of course, invisible to others; however, language provides a means for expressing thoughts and feelings, for receiving messages from others about their inner experience, and for sharing ideas about the nature of psychological life in general. Language development is associated with the ability to infer others' beliefs and emotions among normally developing preschool children and children with autism (e.g., Astington and Jenkins 1999; Happe 1995; Jenkins and Astington 1996; Lind and Bowler 2009; Milligan et al. 2007; Pons et al. 2003; Slade and Ruffman 2005). For example Jenkins and Astington (1996), reported that among 3- to 5-year-old children, general language ability and verbal memory were correlated with performance on false belief tasks. In a subsequent meta-analysis of 104 studies, Milligan et al. (2007) found that for children under seven years of age, general language ability is correlated with false belief performance, even when controlling for age, and that earlier language assessments predict later false belief performance more strongly than earlier false belief performance predicts later language ability.

During early childhood, family discussions of mental states, involving mothers and/or siblings, are associated with more advanced understanding of emotion and belief (Adrian et al. 2005; Dunn and Brown 1993; Dunn et al. 1991a; Peterson and Slaughter 2003; Ruffman et al. 2002; Sabbagh and Callanan 1998; Turnbull and Carpendale 2001). However, when mothers comment on their children's mental states, the appropriateness of mothers' mental state references, not just the frequency, seems to make a difference. Meins and Fernyhough (1999) identified maternal "mind-mindedness" as "the proclivity to treat one's child as an individual with a mind from an early age" (p. 364). Measures of maternal mind-mindedness include a mother responding to her infant's direction of gaze by looking at, touching, picking up, naming, or describing the object her infant is looking at (Meins et al. 2003). To investigate the relation between early maternal mind-mindedness and later understanding of mental life, Meins et al. (2003) assessed maternal mind-mindedness when infants were 6 months old and again when children were 48 months old. Appropriate mind-related comments were distinguished from inappropriate mind-related comments. Appropriate comments appeared to be an accurate reading of the child's mental state or were related to the infants' activity, whereas inappropriate comments appeared unrelated to the infants' current mental state or activity. At 45–48 months of age, the researchers also assessed children's understanding of false beliefs and the appearance-reality distinction. When children reached 55 months, their understanding of the stream of consciousness was assessed. Maternal mind-mindedness was stable from infancy to childhood, but early maternal mind-mindedness was predictive of children's later social cognition. In particular, mothers' appropriate mind-related comments at 6 months were related to children's understanding of false beliefs and the appearance-reality distinction at 4 years and to children's understanding of the stream of consciousness at 4 and half years.

Conversations with friends also are an important context for mental state talk. In fact, Brown et al. (1996) found that among 47-month-olds, references to mental states were more common in conversations with siblings and friends than with mothers. In a longitudinal study, Hughes and Dunn (1998) reported that children who talked about mental states more frequently at 47 months performed better on tests of false belief understanding 13 months later. Furthermore, mental state talk with friends is more frequent while children are pretending (Hughes and Dunn 1997), and participating in shared pretend play is associated with successful perspective-taking among preschool children (Brown et al. 1996). Child-sibling and child-friend dyads that used more mental state terms had more cooperative interactions, and children who used more mental state terms with talking with siblings and friends demonstrated better understanding of another person's false belief.

In a behavioral genetic study of 5-year-old twins, Hughes et al. (2005) found evidence that environmental factors explained most of the variance in children's mental state understanding. Hughes et al. speculated that maternal speech and sibling interactions might contribute to this relationship. Intervention studies also indicate that adult-child discussions influence children's performance on false belief tasks (e.g., Appleton and Reddy 1996; Knoll and Charman 2000; Lohman and Tomasello 2003; Slaughter and Gopnik 1996). Many studies of conversation and children's mental state understanding have examined children approximately 3- and 4-years of age. In addition, de Rosnay et al. (2004) found that mothers' use of psychological rather than behavioral descriptions of their children was related to 4- to 6-year-olds' correct attributions of both false beliefs and emotions based on false beliefs. Based on this finding, de Rosnay et al. (2004) suggest that maternal speech continues to influence children's understanding of mental states beyond 4-year-olds' basic understanding of false beliefs.

Studies of deaf children also indicate that linguistic experience is related to social understanding. Deaf children of hearing parents are delayed in understanding knowledge and false belief (e.g., Peterson and Siegal 1995; Peterson et al. 2005). The age at which deaf children first begin to sign, influences children's subsequent performance on measures of mental state reasoning. Assessing false belief understanding with a pictorial task, Woolfe et al. (2002) compared native signers of British Sign Language, who learned the language from signing family members, and late signing children who first began signing when they entered school. Among children 4- to 9-years of age, the native signers demonstrated better false belief understanding than did the late signers, and the native signers also performed comparably to hearing children. Meristo et al. (2007) found that for both native signers and late signers the medium of academic instruction children experienced at school was related to proficiency in reasoning about true and false beliefs. Children receiving instruction in both Italian Sign Language and spoken Italian performed better than did children receiving in instruction in spoken Italian alone. Likewise, among children aged 6- to 16-years, native signers of Estonian Sign Language who were instructed in both spoken Estonian and Estonian Sign Language performed better than did their counterparts attending oralist schools on measures reasoning about second-order beliefs (i.e., Person A's beliefs about what Person B thinks) and relations among belief, desire, and emotion. Thus, communicative experience continues to influence social cognitive ability even at later ages as children advance beyond basic mental state reasoning.

Language and conversation have been implicated as important factors in the development of children's understanding of mental states. These findings raise questions about the means by which linguistic experience may influence children's social cognitive abilities. Harris et al. (2005) identified three ways in which language may contribute to children's understanding of the mind. First, semantic development may facilitate children's understanding of mental states. Parents, siblings, and other conversational partners may refer to mental states, using terms such as "know", "think", "want", "see", etc. Learning this mental state vocabulary focuses children's attention on internal states. As a result, children may become increasingly aware of both their own and others' knowledge, ignorance, beliefs, and desires. Second, the distinctive syntax of mental state talk may help children understand the nature of mental states. De Villiers and Pyers (2002) argued that because mental state verbs can have an embedded proposition, references to mental states provide a syntactic cue to the content of another person's mind. For example, in the sentence, "Sarah thought the earth was flat", the embedded proposition "the earth was flat" refers to the content of Sarah's belief. According to De Villiers and Pyers, mastering the syntax of such sentences facilitates children's understanding of differences in perspective. Their longitudinal study of children ages 3- to 5-years of age supported this position. However, on the contrary, Harris et al. (2005) cite two studies that failed to find a relation between syntactic development and false belief understanding among children learning German (Perner et al. 2003) or Cantonese (Cheung et al. 2004). Evidence for syntactic influence remains mixed.

A third possibility is that conversational pragmatics alert children to differences in perspective. Harris et al. (2005) suggest that by articulating different viewpoints, discussions of thoughts and feelings inform children's understanding of mental states. That is, a parent's sensitivity to internal states, rather than specific vocabulary terms or syntactic forms, may aid children's social understanding. Carpendale and Lewis (2004) also view conversation as involving more than direct transmission of mental concepts. Rather, they argue that through communication about beliefs, children gradually construct an understanding of belief.

4.3.4 Implications for Children's Understanding Cognitive Activities

Findings that social interaction is related to young children's understanding of mental states raise the question of whether social interaction is similarly related to older children's understanding of cognitive activities. By the time children are 5- or 6-years old, they have had a good deal of social experience, including many sorts of interactions with a range of partners from peers to adults. By this age children already possess a vocabulary with many mental state terms and have attained basic syntactic and pragmatic competence. Nevertheless, from middle childhood through adolescence, children's social interactions, language, and conversational abilities may continue to grow more subtle, varied, and complex. At the same time, older children and adolescents may be increasingly motivated to express their psychological and social experiences to others. Children's changing social worlds may provide experiences that inform a more advanced understanding of cognitive functioning.

More specifically, mentalistic discourse might be related to children's understanding of cognitive activities in three ways. First, during middle childhood both adults and peers may explicitly refer to processes such as attention, memory, and reasoning. For instance, after an adult explained the efficacy of two learning strategies children showed both improved strategy selection for a pair-associated learning task and understanding of the differential effectiveness of the strategies (Ghatala et al. 1986). Naturally occurring conversational references to cognitive activities also might inform children's concepts of cognition. Second, rather than refer directly to cognitive processes, adults and peers may discuss mental states. Discussions of mental states may stimulate reflection on or inferences about the cognitive activities that influence them. Third, early childhood mental state talk might indirectly influence learning about cognition during middle childhood. That is, early mental state talk may facilitate children's understanding of mental states which in turn provides a foundation for further learning about psychological functioning at later ages. These three possibilities remain to be investigated. Also, even when social partners do not explicitly discuss mental states or cognitive processes, conversational interactions that confront children with differences in perspective may motivate attention to cognitive processes as a possible means of explaining the origin of conflicting views.

Documenting patterns of discourse about psychological matters from middle childhood through adolescence may provide insight into the growth of children's psychological understanding. In addition to conversations with parents, conversations with peers and teachers may make important contributions to social cognitive development. Furthermore, children's own expressions of thoughts about mental functioning may serve as a window into their changing conceptions of cognitive activities. Distinguishing among different aspects of children's knowledge of cognitive functioning may be useful for investigation of conversational influences on development. Knowledge of the occurrence of cognitive activities, knowledge of the organization of cognitive activities, and epistemological thought each may be influenced by conversational experience; however, it is possible that the nature of conversational influence may vary for these different aspects of children's understanding of cognition.

4.4 Formal Education, Metacognitive Knowledge and Epistemological Development

A great many advances in understanding cognition occur during children's school years, from elementary school through high school. Through the cultural institution of formal education, children participate in both pedagogical and social exchanges that differ in some key ways from experiences within the family or peer group away from school. Because formal education is designed to promote cognitive goals—learning, reasoning, problem solving, etc., the academic setting may be a uniquely important context for the development of children's understanding of cognition.

As socio-cultural theories indicate, the role of social experience in cognitive development is not limited to transmission of information and ideas from one individual to another (Rogoff 1990; Tomasello 1999). By observing other person's actions and participating in social interactions, children may learn about cognitive activities through processes of intersubjectivity, introspection, and explanation. Initially these insights may be fleeting experiences that occur during an ongoing social exchange. With repeated experience, as well as reflection on past social exchanges, children's understanding may be consolidated into more stable and lasting conceptual knowledge. Tomasello (1999) speculated that as children transition from early to middle childhood, adults instruct and regulate children by commenting on thoughts and beliefs. Children's internalization of this meta discouse leads children to reflect on their own thoughts and facilitates metacognitive development. As Tomasello notes, in many societies deliberate instruction becomes common as children reach 5- to 7-years of age. This emerging instructional discourse may constitute a new form of social interaction stimulating discussion of and reflection on cognitive activities. Thus, in addition to conversations with parents, siblings, and peers, the experience of formal education may influence children's understanding of the mind.

Classroom settings may provide a variety of experiences that stimulate insight into cognitive activity. Teachers may engage in direct metacognitive instruction by teaching children about the utility of particular strategies, helping children to practice them, or encouraging children to engage in monitoring and evaluation of their efforts. During less formal conversations teachers may comment on a student's thought processes or refer to the teacher's own thinking. Lesson plans in science, history, and other disciplines may include the presentation of contrasting views on an issue, and also may include discussions of the reasoning and thought processes of scientists, politicians, or other current or historical figures. Classroom debates may involve children more directly with differing perspectives, the justification of their own position, and critical evaluation of opposing views. In addition, partners in collaborative problem solving may anticipate and comment on each others' thoughts.

Schraw (1998) identified four general ways that classroom settings may improve metacognition: (a) promoting awareness of the importance of metacognition, (b) improving knowledge of cognition, (c) improving regulation of cognition, and (d) fostering environments that promote metacognitive awareness. According to Schraw, teachers can facilitate metacognitive development by discussing the importance of metacognition for learning, modeling their own metacognition for students, allowing time for group discussion, and creating an environment than emphasizes mastery rather than performance. Instruction and training have been shown to be effective for improving both children's and adults' metacognitive knowledge and monitoring (e.g., Cross and Paris 1988; Hacker et al. 2009; Palinscar and Brown 1984; Waters and Schneider 2009).

Educational experience also is related to epistemological development. For example, Kuhn et al. (1988) reported advances in epistemological reasoning with increased age and education level. The most advanced levels of epistemological thought, exhibiting rationalist or evaluativist reasoning, began to appear in late adolescence among twelfth-grade students and became more frequent among adults and graduate students. Mansfield and Clinchy (2002) reported increased awareness of subjectivity between ages 10- and 16-years of age, and Chandler et al. (1990) found developmental progress from between 8th- and 12th-grade. Moreover, educational curricula and practices aimed at promoting critical thinking and epistemological growth appear to be effective. Thus, Clinchy et al. (1977) reported epistemological advances among students at a progressive high school from their sophomore to senior years. Educational programs can bring about epistemological change even during late childhood. Comparing a traditional approach to science education with a program designed to teach a constructivist perspective, Smith, Maclin, Houghton, and Hennessy (2000) found that sixth-grade students' views of science differed depending on which approach they had experienced. Students in the more traditional classroom viewed science as a steady accumulation of facts. This view, termed a "knowledge unproblematic" epistemology of science, is typical of elementary and middle-school students (Carey and Smith 1993). In contrast, students who experienced the constructivist pedagogy, which involved actively developing ideas, and testing and revising their ideas through collaborative inquiry and discussion, developed a constructivist epistemology of science. That is, these students showed greater awareness of the impact of scientists' ideas in the process of scientific inquiry and knowledge acquisition.

I have organized the research literature on children's understanding of mental functioning by distinguishing among three forms of knowledge of cognitive activities: (a) occurrence knowledge, (b) organizational knowledge, and (c) epistemological thought. Occurrence knowledge, organizational knowledge, and epistemological thought may each be influenced by formal educational experience, and, in turn, the emergence of each level of knowledge may facilitate advances in children's participation and learning from academic discourse; however, the relation between patterns of academic discourse and the development of these three forms of knowledge of cognition remains to be investigated.

4.5 Cultural Variation

Both social processes and beliefs about cognitive functioning may vary across cultures. Many cross-cultural variations in folk psychologies have been documented, though the evidence remains fragmentary (see Lillard (1998) for a review). Regarding children's conceptions of cognitive activities, three types of variation are of particular interest: (a) variations in the socialization of children's understanding of mental processes, (b) variations in societal conceptions of the mind and cognition, and (c) variations in the developmental timing of core concepts. Although a body of research on cultural differences in the development of young children's conception of beliefs has emerged in recent years (e.g., Callaghan et al. 2005; Tardif et al. 2005; Vinden 1996), direct evidence concerning cultural differences in the content and development of concepts of specific cognitive processes during middle and late childhood appears to be lacking. Because cross-cultural studies of young children's false belief understanding may suggest some directions for investigations of children's understanding of cognitive activities, I will summarize some of this research briefly.

Several studies have examined the developmental timing of children's understanding of beliefs and other mental states. Cross-cultural comparisons have been made for children's understanding the appearance-reality distinction and false beliefs. In both the United States and China children begin to understand that an object's appearance may differ from its reality around 4 years of age (Flavell et al. 1983), and around 6 years of age children in the United States, Britain, and Japan understand that a person's facial expression may contrast with the person's emotion (Harris and Gross 1988). Among the Baka of Cameroon, 4- and 5-year-olds understand false belief, just as is the case in Austria, Britain, the United States, and other western countries (Avis and Harris 1991). However, Vinden (1996) reported that in Peru 4- to 8-year-old Quechua children performed poorly on false belief tasks. Interestingly, Quechua adults have a large vocabulary for describing appearances, and Vinden found that Quechua children typically understood the appearance-reality distinction. In a meta-analysis, Liu et al. (2008) surveyed studies of false belief understanding from the United States, Canada, mainland China, and Hong Kong. Although they reported parallels in developmental trajectories across the four locales Liu et al. (2008), also found differences in developmental timing, including two-year difference with children in mainland China achieving false belief understanding ahead of those in Hong Kong.

Cultures vary in the extent to which mental states are discussed. Whereas English contains thousands of mental state terms Howell (1981), reported fewer than three dozen such words among the Chewong of Malaysia. Likewise, the Gussii of Kenya, the Baining of Papua New Guinea, and Samoans prefer not to comment on mental states or reasons for actions (Lillard 1998), and the Quechua of Peru refer to thoughts and beliefs indirectly (Vinden 1996). Likewise, compared to European American parents, Chinese parents mention mental states less frequently when discussing past events with young children (Wang and Fivush 2005).

Therefore, children in many cultures do not seem to experience the same discussions of mental states that are associated with social cognitive development in the United States and Britain. Understanding of mental states and cognitive processes must develop via other routes, or differ substantially in content and centrality. Lu et al. (2008) examined the possibility of alternative developmental pathways across cultures. Whereas mental state talk during mother–child conversation is associated with understanding of mental states in early childhood in studies conducted in the United States and Britain, the lower frequency of mental state talk during parent–child conversations in China makes it unlikely that references to mental states are a major influence on Chinese children's understanding of the mind. Instead, Lu et al. (2008) showed the significance of references to other people for Chinese children's understanding of mental states. Although Chinese children talk about mental states less frequently than do European American children, Chinese children often refer to other people and social interaction in their autobiographical recall (Wang 2004). Furthermore, Chinese mothers often mention shared activities and behavior of others when discussing past events with young children (Wang and Fivush 2005). In both a correlational study and a training study, Lu et al. (2008) found that among Chinese 3- and 4-year-olds increases in references to others during autobiographical recall over the span of a year were related to improved performance on false belief tasks, and children who were trained to talk about others during storytelling also showed improved performance. Lu et al. (2008) concluded that autobiographical recall is an important context for theory of mind development, but among Chinese families discussing others's external actions and social interactions, rather than talking about the child's thoughts and feelings, may facilitate social understanding. Thus, there may be different developmental pathways across cultures. In a comparison of Korean-American and Anglo-American families, Vinden (2001) made a similar point. She found that authoritarian parenting was negatively correlated with false belief understanding among Anglo-American, but not Korean-American, 5-year-olds. Vinden concluded that the same outcome can be reached by different means.

Although there are developmental similarities across many cultures, there also are variations in the development of children's understanding of mental states. In addition, there is evidence for cultural differences in epistemological thought during adolescence and adulthood (Karabenick and Moosa 2005; Qian and Pan 2002). Cross-cultural comparisons of children's understanding of cognitive activities such as attention, memory, and reasoning remain to be conducted. Cross-cultural studies of cognitive monitoring, and the social contexts in which it occurs, also would be valuable.

4.6 Summary

Studies of social influences on children's social cognitive development have concentrated on the growth of children's early mental state reasoning. Conversational interactions with parents, siblings, and peers appear to be related to young children's understanding of beliefs and emotions. In addition, there may be cultural variations in the development of mental state reasoning. Although these results suggest the possibility that social and cultural factors may guide the development of children's conceptual knowledge of cognitive activities, this possibility has not been investigated empirically. The present model suggests that processes of observation, social interaction, and participation in cultural activities are contexts that facilitate the emergence of knowledge about cognitive functioning. However, developmental relations between children's social experience and children's knowledge of cognitive activities remain to be investigated. Future studies should investigate both social influences on children's knowledge of cognition and the influence of changes in children's knowledge of cognition on children's social experience.

References

Adrian, J. E., Clemente, R. A., Villanueva, L., & Rieffe, C. (2005). Parent-child picture-book reading, mothers' mental state language, and children's theory of mind. *Journal of Child Language, 32*, 673–686.

Appleton, M., & Reddy, V. (1996). Teaching three year-olds to pass false-belief tests: A conversational approach. *Social Development, 5*, 275–291.

Astingon, J. W., & Jenkins, J. M. (1999). A longitudinal study of the relation between language and theory of mind development. *Developmental Psychology, 35*, 1311–1320.

Avis, J., & Harris, P. L. (1991). Belief-desire reasoning among Baka children: Evidence for a universal conception of mind. *Child Development, 62*, 460–467.

Bem, D. J. (1972). Self-perception theory. In L. Berkowitz (Ed.), *Advances in experimental social psychology* (Vol. 6, pp. 1–62). New York: Academic.

Brown, J. R., Donelan-McCall, N., & Dunn, J. (1996). Why talk about mental states? The significance of children's conversations with friends, siblings, and mothers. *Child Development, 67*, 836–849.

Callaghan, T., Rochat, P., Lillard, A., Claux, M. L., Odden, H., Itakura, S., et al. (2005). Synchrony in the onset of mental-state reasoning: Evidence from five cultures. *Psychological Science, 16*, 378–384.

Carey, S., & Smith, C. (1993). On understanding the nature of scientific knowledge. *Educational Psychologist, 28*, 235–251.

Carlson, S. M., & Moses, L. J. (2001). Individual differences in inhibitory control and children's theory of mind. *Child Development, 72*, 1032–1053.

Carpendale, J. I. M., & Lewis, C. (2004). Constructing an understanding of mind: The development of children's social understanding within social interaction. *Behavioral and Brain Sciences, 27*, 79–151.

Chandler, M. J., Boyes, M. C., & Ball, L. (1990). Relativism and stations of epistemic doubt. *Journal of Experimental Child Psychology, 50*, 370–395.

Chapman, M. (1991). The epistemic triangle: Operative and communicative components of cognitive development. In M. J. Chandler & M. Chapman (Eds.), *Criteria for competence: Controversies in the conceptualization and assessment of children's abilities* (pp. 209–228). Hillsdale: Lawrence Erlbaum Associates.

Cheung, H., Hsuan-Chi, C., Creed, N., Ng, L., Wang, S. P., & Mo, L. (2004). Relative roles of general and complementation language in theory of mind development: Evidence from Cantonese and English. *Child Development, 75*, 1155–1170.

Clinchy, B., Lief, J., & Young, P. (1977). Epistemological and moral development in girls from a traditional and a progressive high school. *Journal of Educational Psychology, 69*, 337–343.

Cross, D. R., & Paris, S. G. (1988). Developmental and instructional analysis of children's metacognition and reading comprehension. *Journal of Educational Psychology, 80*, 131–142.

Cutting, A. L., & Dunn, J. (1999). Theory of mind, emotion understanding, language, and family background: Individual differences and interrelations. *Child Development, 70*, 853–865.

de Rosnay, M., Pons, R., Harris, P. L., & Morrell, J. M. B. (2004). A lag between understanding false belief and emotion attribution in young children: Relationships with linguistic ability and mothers' mental-state language. *British Journal of Developmental Psychology, 22*, 197–218.

de Villers, J. G., & Pyers, J. E. (2002). Complements to cognition: A longitudinal study of the relationship between complex syntax and false-belief-understanding. *Cognitive Development, 17*, 1037–1060.

Dunn, J., & Brown, J. (1993). Early conversations about causality: Content, pragmatics, and developmental change. *British Journal of Developmental Psychology, 11*, 107–123.

Dunn, J., Brown, J., & Beardsall, L. (1991a). Family talk about feeling states and children's later understanding of others' emotions. *Developmental Psychology, 27*, 448–455.

Dunn, J., Brown, J., Slomkowski, C., Tesla, C., & Youngblade, L. (1991b). Young children's understanding of other people's feelings and beliefs: Individual differences and their antecedents. *Child Development, 62*, 1352–1366.

Flavell, J. H., Zhang, X.-D., Zou, H., Dong, Q., & Qi, S. (1983). A comparison between the development of the appearance-reality distinction in the People's Republic of China and the United States. *Cognitive Psychology, 15*, 459–466.

Ghatala, E. S., Levin, J. R., Pressley, M., & Goodwin, D. (1986). A componential analysis of the effects of derived and supplied strategy-utility information on children's strategy selections. *Journal of Experimental Child Psychology, 41*, 76–92.

Gopnik, A. (1993). How we know our minds: The illusion of first-person knowledge of intentionality. *Behavioral and Brain Sciences, 16*, 1–14.

Gopnik, A., & Wellman, H. M. (1992). Why the child's theory of mind really is a theory. *Mind and Language, 7*, 145–171.

Hacker, D. J., Dunlosky, J., & Graesser, A. C. (2009). *Handbook of metacognition in education.* New York: Taylor and Francis Group.

Happe', F. G. E. (1995). The role of age and verbal ability in the theory of mind task performance of subjects with autism. *Child Development, 66*, 843–855.

Harris, P. L., & Gross, D. (1988). Children's understanding of real and apparent emotion. In J. W. Astington, P. L. Harris, & D. R. Olson (Eds.), *Developing theories of mind* (pp. 295–314). New York: Cambridge University Press.

Harris, P. L., de Rosnay, M., & Pons, F. (2005). Language and children's understanding of mental states. *Current Directions in Psychological Science, 14*, 69–73.

Howell, S. (1981). Rules not words. In P. Heelas & A. Lock (Eds.), *Indigenous psychologies* (pp. 133–144). New York: Academic.

Hughes, C., & Dunn, J. (1997). Pretend you didn't know: Preschoolers' talk about mental states in pretend play. *Cognitive Development, 12*, 477–499.

Hughes, C., & Dunn, J. (1998). Understanding mind and emotion: Longitudinal associations with mental-state talk between young friends. *Developmental Psychology, 34*, 1026–1037.

Hughes, C., Jaffee, S. R., Happe, F., Taylor, A., Caspi, A., & Moffitt, T. E. (2005). Origins of individual differences in theory of mind: From nature to nurture? *Child Development, 76*, 356–370.

Jenkins, J. M., & Astington, J. W. (1996). Cognitive factors and family structure associated with theory of mind development in young children. *Developmental Psychology, 32*, 70–78.

Karabenick, S., & Moosa, S. (2005). Culture and personal epistemology: U.S. and Middle Eastern students' beliefs about scientific knowledge and knowing. *Social Psychology of Education, 8*, 375–393.

Knoll, M., & Charman, T. (2000). Teaching false belief and visual perspective taking skills in young children: Can a theory of mind be trained? *Child Study Journal, 30,* 273–304.

Kuhn, D., Amsel, E., & O'Loughlin, M. (1988). *The development of scientific thinking skills.* San Diego: Academic.

Laible, D., & Thompson, R. (1998). Attachment and emotional understanding in preschool children. *Developmental Psychology, 34,* 1038–1045.

Lewis, C., Freeman, N. H., Kyriakidou, C., Maridaki-Kassotaki, K., & Berridge, D. M. (1996). Social influences on false belief access: Specific sibling influences or general apprenticeship? *Child Development, 67,* 2930–2947.

Lillard, A. (1998). Ethnopsychologies: Cultural variations in theories of mind. *Psychological Bulletin, 123,* 3–32.

Lillard, A. (1999). Developing a cultural theory of mind: The CIAO approach. *Current Directions in Psychological Science, 8,* 57–61.

Lillard, A. S., & Flavell, J. H. (1990). Young children's preference for mental state versus behavioral descriptions of human action. *Child Development, 61,* 731–741.

Lind, S. E., & Bolwer, D. M. (2009). Language and theory of mind in autism spectrum disorder: The relationship between complement syntax and false belief task performance. *Journal of Autism and Developmental Disorders, 39,* 929–937.

Liu, D., Wellman, H. M., Tardif, T., & Sabbagh, M. A. (2008). Theory of mind development in Chinese children: A meta-analysis of false-belief understanding across cultures and languages. *Developmental Psychology, 44,* 523–531.

Lohman, H., & Tomasello, M. (2003). The role of language in the development of false belief understanding: A training study. *Child Development, 74,* 1130–1144.

Lu, H., Su, Y., & Wang, Q. (2008). Talking about others facilitates theory of mind in Chinese preschoolers. *Developmental Psychology, 44,* 1726–1736.

Mansfield, A., & Clinchy, B. M. (2002). Toward the integration of objectivity and subjectivity: Epistemological development from 10 to 16. *New Ideas in Psychology, 20,* 225–262.

McGivern, J. E., Levin, J. R., Pressley, M., & Ghatala, E. S. (1990). A developmental study of memory monitoring and strategy selection. *Contemporary Educational Psychology, 15,* 103–115.

Meins, E., & Fernyhough, C. (1999). Linguistic acquisitional style and mentalising development: The role of maternal mind-mindedness. *Cognitive Development, 14,* 363–380.

Meins, E., Fernyhough, C., Russell, J., & Clark-Carter, D. (1998). Security of attachment as a predictor of symbolic and mentalising abilities: A longitudinal study. *Social Development, 7,* 1–24.

Meins, E., Fernyhough, C., Wainwright, R., Clark-Carter, D., Das Gupta, M., Fradley, E., et al. (2003). Pathways to understanding mind: Construct validity and predictive validity of maternal mind-mindedness. *Child Development, 74,* 1194–1211.

Meltzoff, A. N., & Moore, M. K. (1997). Explaining facial imitation: A theoretical model. *Early Development and Parenting, 6,* 179–192.

Meristo, M., Falkman, K. W., Hjelmquist, E., Tedoldi, M., Surian, L., & Siegal, M. (2007). Language access and theory of mind reasoning: Evidence from deaf children in bilingual and oralist environments. *Developmental Psychology, 43,* 1156–1169.

Miller, P. H., & Aloise, P. A. (1989). Young children's understanding of the psychological causes of behavior: A review. *Child Development, 60,* 257–285.

Milligan, K., Astington, J. W., & Dack, L. A. (2007). Language and theory of mind: Meta-analysis of the relation between language ability and false-belief understanding. *Child Development, 78,* 622–646.

Moore, C. (2006). *The development of commonsense psychology.* Mahwah: Lawrence Erlbaum Associates.

Palincsar, A. S., & Brown, A. (1984). Reciprocal teaching of comprehension-fostering and comprehension-monitoring activities. *Cognition and Instruction, 1,* 117–175.

Pears, K. C., & Moses, L. J. (2003). Demographics, parenting, and theory of mind in preschool children. *Social Development, 12,* 1–20.

Perner, J., Ruffman, T., & Leekam, S. R. (1994). Theory of mind is contagious: You catch it from your sibs. *Child Development, 65,* 1228–1238.

Perner, J., Sprung, M., Zauner, P., & Haider, H. (2003). Want that is understood well before say that, think that, and false belief: A test of deVilliers' linguistic determinism on German-speaking children. *Child Development, 74,* 179–188.

Peterson, C. C., & Siegal, M. (1995). Deafness, conversation, and theory of mind. *Journal of Child Psychology and Psychiatry, 36,* 459–474.

Peterson, C. C., & Slaughter, V. (2003). Opening windows into the mind: Mothers' preferences for mental state explanations and children's theory of mind. *Cognitive Development, 18,* 399–429.

Peterson, C. C., Wellman, H. M., & Liu, D. (2005). Steps in theory-of-mind development for children with deafness or autism. *Child Development, 76,* 502–517.

Pillow, B. H., & Lovett, S. B. (1998). He forgot: Young children's use of cognitive explanations for another person's mistakes. *Merrill-Palmer Quarterly, 44,* 378–403.

Pillow, B. H., Mash, C., Aloian, S., & Hill, V. (2002). Facilitating children's understanding of misinterpretation: Explanatory efforts and improvements in perspective-taking. *The Journal of Genetic Psychology, 163,* 133–148.

Pons, F., Harris, P. L., & deRosnay, M. (2003). Emotion comprehension between 3 and 11 years: Developmental periods and hierarchical organization. *European Journal of Developmental Psychology, 2,* 127–152.

Qian, G., & Pan, J. (2002). A comparison of epistemological beliefs and learning from science text between American and Chinese high school students. In B. K. Hofer & P. R. Pintrich (Eds.), *Personal epistemology: The psychology of beliefs about knowledge and knowing* (pp. 365–385). Mahwah: Lawrence Erlbaum Associates.

Rogoff, B. (1990). *Apprenticeship in thinking: Cognitive development in social context.* New York: Oxford University Press.

Ruffman, T., Perner, J., Naito, M., Parkin, L., & Clements, W. A. (1998). Older (but not younger) siblings facilitate false belief understanding. *Developmental Psychology, 34,* 161–174.

Ruffman, T., Perner, J., & Parkin, L. (1999). How parenting style affects false belief understanding. *Social Development, 8,* 395–411.

Ruffman, T., Slade, L., & Crowe, E. (2002). The relation between children's and mothers' mental state language and theory-of-mind understanding. *Child Development, 73,* 734–751.

Sabbagh, M. A., & Callanan, M. A. (1998). Metarepresentation in action: 3-, 4-, and 5-year-olds' developing theories of mind in parent-child conversations. *Developmental Psychology, 34,* 491–502.

Schraw, G. (1998). Promoting general metacognitive awareness. *Instructional Science, 26,* 113–125.

Slade, L., & Ruffman, T. (2005). How language does (and does not) relate to theory of mind: A longitudinal study of syntax, semantics, working memory, and false belief. *British Journal of Developmental Psychology, 23,* 117–141.

Slaughter, V., & Gopnik, A. (1996). Conceptual coherence in the child's theory of mind: Training children to understand belief. *Child Development, 67,* 2967–2988.

Smith, C. L., Maclin, D., Houghton, C., & Hennessy, M. G. (2000). Sixth-grade students' epistemologies of science: The impact of school science experiences on epistemological development. *Cognition and Instruction, 18,* 349–342.

Tardif, T., Wellman, H. M., Fung, K. Y. F., Liu, D., & Fang, F. (2005). Preschoolers' understanding of knowing-that and knowing-how in the United States and Hong Kong. *Developmental Psychology, 41,* 562–573.

Tomasello, M. (1999). *The cultural origins of human cognition.* Cambridge: Harvard University Press.

Trevarthen, C., & Aitken, K. J. (2001). Infant intersubjectivity: Research, theory, and clinical applications. *Journal of Child Psychology and Psychiatry and Allied Disciplines, 42,* 3–48.

Turnbull, W., & Carpendale, J. I. M. (2001). Talk and the development of social understanding. *Early Education and Development, 12,* 455–477.

Vinden, P. (1996). Junin Quechua children's understanding of mind. *Child Development, 67,* 1707–1716.

Vinden, P. (2001). Parenting attitudes and children's understanding of mind: A comparison of Korean-American and Anglo-American families. *Cognitive Development, 16,* 793–809.

Wang, Q. (2004). The emergence of cultural self-construct: Autobiographical memory and self-description in American and Chinese children. *Developmental Psychology, 40,* 3–15.

Wang, Q., & Fivush, R. (2005). Mother-child conversations of emotionally salient events: Exploring the functions of emotional reminiscing in European-American and Chinese families. *Social Development, 14,* 473–495.

Waters, H. S., & Schneider, W. (2009). *Metacognition, strategy use, and instruction.* New York: Guilford Press.

Wellman, H. M. (1990). *The child's theory of mind.* Cambridge: MIT Press.

Woolfe, T., Want, S. T., & Siegal, M. (2002). Signposts to development: Theory of mind in deaf children. *Child Development, 73,* 768–778.

Chapter 5
Patterns of Influence Among Phenomenological Awareness, Social Experience and Conceptual Knowledge

Abstract Proposals concerning patterns of influence among children's developing conceptual knowledge of cognition, children's phenomenological awareness of their own cognitive functioning, and social experience are further elaborated. Relations of reciprocal influence between conceptual knowledge and cognitive monitoring, conceptual knowledge and social experience, and social experience and cognitive monitoring are described. In addition, possible developmental mechanisms underlying the acquisition of knowledge about cognitive activities are considered, focusing on the issue of domain-specific modules versus domain-general learning processes. As children learn about cognition, general learning processes, particularly pattern recognition and executive function, may help them to integrate their mental state concepts with information available through first-person phenomenological experience and social experience.

Knowledge of cognition appears fairly early and increases throughout childhood and adolescence, into adulthood (as discussed in Chap. 2). During the elementary school years, children learn about the occurrence of a wide range of cognitive activities, including attention, memory, the stream of consciousness, reasoning, and emotional cueing of thoughts. Children's knowledge of cognition begins to grow more abstract during late childhood, as they start to organize their concepts of cognition in terms of dimensions such as information processing role and certainty. Adolescents and adults develop personal epistemologies—yet more abstract conceptions of the nature of knowledge and the relation between mind and reality. The development of concepts of cognition raises the question of how children learn about cognitive functioning. I proposed in Chap. 1 that concepts of cognition are informed by first-person phenomenological awareness and social experience, and that, in turn, conceptual knowledge of the mind is used to interpret the cues available from those sources. The empirical literatures on cognitive monitoring and social cognitive development, reviewed in Chaps. 3 and 4 respectively, indicate that both phenomenological awareness of cognitive

B. H. Pillow, *Children's Discovery of the Active Mind,*
SpringerBriefs in Child Development, DOI: 10.1007/978-1-4614-2248-8_5,
© Bradford H. Pillow 2012

functioning and social interaction are available to children as potential sources of information about the occurrence and nature of cognitive activities. Although cognitive monitoring is limited and improves with age, even young children have some ability to monitor their own mental life. Conversation and other social experiences provide guidance regarding the significance of psychological events, both cognitive and affective. Moreover, phenomenological awareness and social experience interact with conceptual knowledge of cognitive activities, as well as with each other. The utility of each source is enhanced when combined with other sources. To more fully characterize the informational base for learning about cognition, it is important to consider patterns of influence among the available sources of input. Below I further examine possible patterns of influence among conceptual knowledge, phenomenological experience, and social experience. Then I consider learning processes that may construct concepts of cognitive activities by operating on these sources of information.

5.1 Phenomenological Awareness and Conceptual Knowledge

Cognitive monitoring and knowledge of cognitive activities influence each other reciprocally (Flavell 1981). Evidence that children learn about cognitive functioning from monitoring their own performance comes from studies of children's strategy knowledge, children's understanding of others' inferences, and children's organization of mental verbs. For example, when prompted to reflect on their performance 10- to 13-year-old children gained explicit knowledge about the effectiveness of word learning strategies (Pressley et al. 1984). Likewise, 6- and 8-year-olds also acquire metacognitive knowledge about strategy effectiveness for paired- associates learning when children are trained to attend to changes in performance following strategy use, attribute changes to strategies, and select the best strategy for the task (Ghatala et al. 1986). A few minutes after children make deductions or guesses, second-grade children's rating of their own level of certainty is correlated with rating another observer's deductions as more certain than guesses (Pillow and Anderson 2006). Thus, memory for children's own level of certainty was related to the conceptual understanding of deduction and guessing that is needed to evaluate another person's certainty. In a study of the organization of knowledge of cognitive activities, Schwanenflugel et al. (1996) found that comprehension monitoring was related to children's organizational knowledge of mental verbs. When asked to judge the similarity of pairs of mental verbs, 8–11 year-old children who were better comprehension monitors differentiated verbs according to their level of certainty more than did children who did not monitor effectively.

According to the proposed framework, monitoring of informational content, source, effort, certainty, and emotion contribute to knowledge of cognitive activities. Children's source monitoring, comprehension monitoring, and memory monitoring have been studied extensively; however, certainty monitoring,

monitoring of effort and difficulty, and emotion monitoring have been studied relatively little. Moreover, the literature often appears fragmented, with different aspects of monitoring being studied at different ages. Comprehensive studies of age-related changes in children's monitoring of different aspects of cognitive functioning are needed, as are detailed studies of children's ability to learn about cognitive activities through monitoring. Theories of consciousness and metacognition (Humphrey 1983, 1986; Koriat 1998; Mandler 2002; Nelson et al. 1998) suggest that introspection on cognitive activities is constructive, requiring interpretation of consciously experienced cues. From this perspective, advances in children's concepts of cognition could lead to changes in monitoring. Thus, the bidirectional relationship between monitoring and metacognitive knowledge also should be investigated over time to determine how knowledge acquisition influences children's phenomenological awareness of cognitive activity.

5.2 Social Experience and Phenomenological Awareness

Social experiences and phenomenological experiences may often occur together. According to socio-cultural theories (Rogoff 1990; Tomasello 1999), social activities such as conversation and shared problem solving encourage perspective-taking and intersubjectivity. Such experiences may also provide a context for relating cognitive monitoring to social information. Feelings of comprehension or confusion may occur while a child is trying to understand a partner's discourse, while a child is attempting to read a document written by another person, or while a child is trying to explain the child's own thoughts to someone else. On the one hand, social interaction can stimulate children's monitoring and interpretation of metacognitive experiences. By providing actions, gestures, and messages for children to comprehend, social partners create the need and opportunity for children to engage in monitoring. On the other hand, children's monitoring efforts may enhance their understanding of their social partners' actions and messages, and thereby facilitate social interaction. For example, an adult's comments about a child's mental states and processes may be made intelligible by the child's monitoring of phenomenological experience. Likewise, monitoring message adequacy and comprehension may enable a child to attribute a peer's failure to comply with a request to communication problems rather than lack of cooperation.

Social interaction and phenomenological awareness of cognitive activities may mesh in various situations. Observation of others' actions and reflection on one's own mental states may co-occur. Alternatively, two individuals working on the same activity, either collaboratively or in parallel, may have similar experiences. For instance, while following a teacher's instructions, a child may feel uncertain about the next step and simultaneously observe a classmate's overt hesitation or quizzical facial expression. Such co-occurrences may increase attention to metacognitive cues and facilitate their interpretation. Adults may also guide children's cognitive monitoring. Salonen et al. (2005) argue that for an optimal match between teacher and learner, teachers must perceive cues indicating students' metacognitive experiences. Such cues include questions, direction of gaze, task engagement, and emotional expressions. According to Salonen et al., teachers' perception of students' metacognitive experiences may guide teachers' instructional behavior. Consequently, metacognition is not purely an individual process, but is part of the social processes involved in the shift from other-regulation to self-regulation.

During collaborative activity children sometimes confuse actions performed by themselves and their partner. Foley et al. (2002) suggest that such source monitoring errors contribute to learning. They found that after working collaboratively with an adult partner toward a shared goal (e.g., making a collage that looked like a model picture), 4-year-old children attributed some of their partner's actions to themselves. According to Foley et al., source monitoring errors occur when a child anticipates another person's actions. Children often recode anticipated actions as their own actual actions. Moreover, they argue that recoding during collaboration promotes internalization of the partner's perspective and learning about the shared task. In support of this view, Ratner et al. (2002) reported that among 5-year-olds, recoding during a collaborative categorization task was related to increases in planning and improvement in individual performance on subsequent categorization tasks. Similar source monitoring errors for an adult's verbal statements about a child's cognitive states and activities could facilitate children's internalization of beliefs about mental functioning. However, this possibility remains to be investigated.

Evidence for adult guidance of cognitive monitoring comes from studies of strategy knowledge. Learning about cognitive strategies is facilitated when adults train children to reflect on children's performance (e.g., Ghatala et al. 1986; Pressley et al. 1984). Similar processes may occur in the classroom as well. For example, based on a classroom study of the interaction between guided inquiry and learning from texts, Palincsar and Magnusson (2001) suggested that teachers facilitate science learning by helping children make connections between information children find in science texts and questions and inferences that occur during children's own first-hand investigations of physical phenomena.

5.3 Social Experience and Conceptual Knowledge

Social experience reciprocally influences conceptual understanding of cognitive activities. First, information about cognitive functioning can be socially transmitted. For example, children can learn about the effectiveness of memory strategies by observing another person engage in them and monitoring that person's performance (McGivern et al. 1990). Reference to cognitive activities during conversation also may be informative. Conversational influence on children's mental state understanding has been demonstrated (e.g., Dunn and Brown 1993; Hughes and Dunn 1997), but, as noted in Chap. 4, similar effects for children's understanding of cognitive activities remain to be investigated. Second, children's conceptual understanding of cognitive activities could influence children's understanding of others. This possibility remains to be investigated.

5.4 Conceptual Knowledge, Phenomenological Awareness and Social Experience

Social experience, phenomenological awareness, and conceptual knowledge also participate in a network of indirect interactions. In one pathway, social experience indirectly influences cognitive monitoring by directly influencing conceptual knowledge. That is, social experience contributes to the development of conceptual knowledge about cognitive activities. This knowledge can in turn impact cognitive monitoring by influencing when children recognize the need to monitor and how children interpret metacognitive cues. Because socially transmitted beliefs about cognition may vary across cultures, the influence of conceptual knowledge on phenomenological awareness of cognitive activities also implies that cultural experience influences cognitive monitoring. Influence in this pathway is bidirectional. Consequently, cognitive monitoring also contributes to the development of conceptual knowledge of cognitive activities, which can then influence how children experience social events. In another pathway, social experience indirectly influences conceptual knowledge by directly affecting cognitive monitoring. That is, social experience facilitates the development of children's cognitive monitoring, and cognitive monitoring contributes to the acquisition of knowledge about cognitive activities. Again, influence in this pathway is bidirectional. Therefore, children's monitoring of their own cognitive states and activities can influence children's understanding of social events. This understanding of social events then may become part of children's conceptual knowledge. These possible pathways of influence imply that phenomenological awareness, conceptual knowledge, and social understanding are intertwined in the development of children's understanding of cognitive activities. Such patterns of influence are consistent with Lillard's (1999) CIAO model of social cognitive development, in which culture, introspection, and detection of analogies between self and other combine to provide a foundation for children's understanding of psychological functioning.

5.5 Processes of Learning

In my efforts to explain how children develop an understanding of cognitive activities, my emphasis has been on identifying sources of information that potentially contribute to children's learning. However, identifying relevant sources of information raises another question—how do children use the available information? That is, what learning process or mechanism enables children to detect information relevant to cognitive functioning, integrate input from diverse sources, and construct concepts of cognition? As with other domains of cognitive development, both innate domain-specific modules and domain-general learning processes have been postulated to account for the development of children's understanding of the mind. These accounts have focused mainly on explaining the origins of young children's understanding of beliefs as mental representations. Domain- specific and domain-general theories will be described briefly below, and their implications for children's understanding of cognitive activities will be discussed.

In his influential theory of modularity, Fodor (1983) characterized modules as innately specified, domain-specific, hardwired, and computationally autonomous, informationally encapsulated systems. Modules operate within highly specific content domains, are innately hardwired rather than formed via learning, function independently in the sense that they do not share processing resources with other systems, and also compute representations in a more or less bottom up fashion, without being influenced by information from other systems or by general knowledge. According to Fodor, perceptual input analyzers are the most likely candidates for modularity. Input analyzers are perceptual modules that the output of sensory transducers as input and compute relatively low-level, uninterpreted, representations of the arrangement of things in the world.

Although Fodor's input analyzers operate at early stages of perceptual processing, others have extended the idea of modularity to social cognitive processes. Leslie (1994) postulated a set of processing modules that enable children to discover three basic properties of animate agents: self-produced movement, goal-directed action, and propositional attitudes. One module, theory of body or ToBy, detects spatio-temporal patterns of movement and interprets them as externally caused or internally caused. In the case of animate agents, this module yields an impression agency. A second module, theory of mind 1, or ToMM1, represents agents as acting in a goal-directed fashion. This module yields the impression that an action is aimed at bringing about a certain state of affairs, without yet attributing a mental representation of a goal to the actor. The third module, theory of mind 2, or ToMM2, represents relations between an agent and a propositional attitude. Consequently, this module enables children to recognize that an agent's action may be a response to a fictional, rather than actual, state of affairs.

Baron-Cohen (1995) offered a modular view of theory of mind development in which the capacity for understanding of other minds depends on a cognitive system consisting of four components: an Intentionality Detector, an Eye-Direction Detector, a Shared Attention Mechanism, and a Theory of Mind Mechanism. The Intentionality Detector is a perceptual device that interprets self-propelled motion in terms of goals and desires. The Eye-Direction Detector is a visual processor that serves three functions: (a) detecting presence of eyes, (b) determining whether eyes are directed toward itself or toward something else, and (c) inferring that eyes see the thing they are looking at. Relying on the output of the Eye-Direction

Detector, the Shared Attention Mechanism builds triadic representations involving the self, another agent, and another object or person. This module represents that the self and other are looking at the same thing, and that both people see that they are both looking at same thing. The Theory of Mind Mechanism, similar to a combination of Leslie's ToMM1 and ToMM2, is a system that infers another person's mental states (i.e., desires, goals, perceptual experiences, thoughts, knowledge, beliefs, etc.) from a person's behavior.

Despite differences in their details, the theories put forth by Leslie and Baron-Cohen share the common feature of a set of hierarchically arranged modules. Each theory begins with perceptual mechanisms that detect physical stimuli, such as patterns of movement or the presence of eyes. These modules produce impressions of agency or intentionality, and this output is used by higher level modules that represent mental states. The modular approach has the advantage of defining a perceptually based starting place for development. While avoiding innate propositional knowledge, these modular theories posit innate processing devices that begin with relatively low-level perceptual inputs and build toward increasingly abstract representations. The modular theories are designed to explain how basic concepts of mental states, especially belief, could be learned from available perceptual information. Although the modules are posited to constrain learning about mental states, they do not appear to directly constrain further learning about cognitive activities. Perhaps they do not need to. That is, once the basic concepts of mental states have been acquired, that conceptual framework may provide the basis for learning about cognitive processes that operate on and transform mental states. General learning processes may be sufficient to take this step, without the need for a module aimed specifically at producing concepts of mental activities. I will return to this idea below, after discussing theories that emphasize general learning processes in the development of children's theory of mind.

In contrast to modularity theories, domain general learning processes have been proposed to account for mental state understanding. Domain general proposals include meta-representational abilities (Perner 1991), executive function (Carlson and Moses 2001), and pattern detection (Moore 2006). According to Perner (1991), for children to understand the mind, they must appreciate the relation between a symbolic representation and its referent. Understanding the nature of representation is necessary for conceptualizing beliefs as representations that stand for situations in the world and may differ from the actual state of affairs. Others have argued that the executive function is related to the development of children's theory of mind. Executive function includes abilities involved in self-regulation, such as directing attention, resisting distraction, controlling motor responses, inhibiting inappropriate responses, and planning. Carlson and Moses (2001) suggested that one aspect of executive function, inhibitory control, is particularly important for children's understanding of beliefs. They view inhibitory control and understanding of beliefs as related in two ways: (a) inhibitory control enables the acquisition of the concept of belief, and (b) inhibitory control facilitates the expression of children's false belief understanding. According to their analysis, false belief understanding requires children to inhibit thoughts about reality in order to think about another person's perspective. By helping children to distance themselves cognitively from their own immediate knowledge of reality, inhibitory control helps children to reflect on other perspectives, and thereby enables the acquisition of the concept of belief. In addition, once children have acquired the concept of belief as a mental representation that may be false, the need to inhibit thoughts about reality when reasoning about another person's perspective continues. Thus, the exercise of inhibitory control remains a factor that influences performance.

In an alternative domain-general theory, Moore (2006) argues that general pattern recognition processes, operating on information available through social interaction, are sufficient to account for the development of children's understanding of other minds. Moore suggests that, beginning in infancy, triadic interactions involving the child, an adult, and an object help children to integrate their first-person experience of their own actions, such as looking at and grasping objects, with the third-person observation of adults engaging in similar acts. As children develop a concept of self, integration of first- and third-person information makes it possible to imagine another person's first-person experience and also think of themselves as an object from a third-person perspective. As a result, children begin to recognize individual differences in perspective. According to Moore, innate, domain-specific processing modules are not needed to account for children's acquisition of a commonsense understanding of other minds. Instead, information from the environment, including the social environment, is structured. Because information is structured, children's ability to detect regularities in temporal contingencies and spatial relations enables recognition of commonly occurring perceptual patterns. Over time, these patterns become integrated into structures, which in turn can be integrated into higher level structures. Through this process of hierarchical integration, abstract concepts can be learned. Thus, Moore views concepts of beliefs and other mental states as being learned from perceptual input with general information processing abilities, rather than dedicated mechanisms for social information.

My purpose here is not to critique domain-specific and domain-general theories, or to evaluate the supporting evidence for each view, but to consider the relevance of these theories for children's learning about cognitive activities. As noted earlier, even if early learning about mental states depends on domain-specific modules, once a basic understanding of mental states has been acquired a further module dedicated to learning about cognitive activities would seem unnecessary. With mental state concepts in place, children could further elaborate their metacognitive by applying general learning processes, such as the pattern recognition abilities emphasized by Moore (2006). Likewise, if metarepresentational competence is critical for understanding knowledge and belief, as Perner (1991) proposed, the resulting representational theory of mind would provide a foundation for learning about cognitive activities. As a developmental precursor, understanding of representation would indirectly facilitate knowledge of cognitive activities, but again, general learning processes might account for the transition from understanding mental states to understanding cognitive activities. Alternatively, if, as

Moore argues, young children's commonsense psychology is derived from general pattern recognition abilities, then those same processes might be responsible for further advances in psychological knowledge. Impressive pattern recognition ability already is apparent during infancy (Saffran 2003). As children's understanding of the mind progresses from early childhood through adolescence, children may extract new patterns from their experience and acquire more advanced concepts.

Therefore, I suspect that, however children's early knowledge of the mind may begin, general learning mechanisms may be enough for learning about cognitive activities by integrating mental state concepts with information available through first-person phenomenological experience and social experience. In addition to pattern recognition processes, executive function also may be important for the development of concepts of cognitive activities. Executive function continues to develop through adolescence. In their review of research on executive function, Best and Miller (2010) concluded that three core components, inhibition, working memory, and attentional shifting, develop on different trajectories. Although all three components develop from early childhood through adolescence, inhibitory abilities improve greatly during early childhood, with less change at later ages, whereas working memory and shifting improve gradually throughout development. Carlson et al. (2002) found that among preschool children inhibitory control predicted false belief understanding, over and above differences in working memory. Likewise, among older children inhibitory control may facilitate awareness of other persons' psychological processes. For instance, setting aside children's own knowledge about an ambiguous event or scene may help children to recognize that another observer could interpret the same information in a different manner. Working memory and shifting focus could also contribute to learning about cognitive activities.

With improvements in monitoring and advances in social development, richer and more complex information about psychological events potentially becomes available. That is, older children may monitor an increasing variety of metacognitive cues, and they may do so with increasing frequency and consistency, and be more likely to recognize the significance of metacognitive experiences. At the same time, older children may participate in increasing sophisticated and subtle social exchanges. Older children's social experiences may be more likely to include psychological discourse. Children also continue to refine and organize their conceptual knowledge of mental functioning, including concepts of mental states and psychological activities. To detect and integrate information derived from cognitive monitoring and social experiences with conceptual knowledge of mental functioning, children would need to shift attention flexibly among multiple inputs, select relevant cues, and have sufficient processing capacity to retain and coordinate the available information. The patterns of influence among phenomenological awareness, social experience, and conceptual knowledge discussed earlier in this chapter include combinations of information from two or three sources. Children and adults might also combine multiple pieces of information from within a single type of source. Two or more different metacognitive cues might be detected, or different aspects of a social event might be noticed and related to each other. Advances in executive function might facilitate processing of multifaceted patterns of information. Consequently, the information available to pattern recognition processes may be enriched by the development of executive function in combination with the growth of cognitive monitoring and social interaction throughout childhood and adolescence.

References

Baron-Cohen, S. (1995). *Mindblindness: An essay on autism and theory of mind*. Cambridge: MIT Press.

Best, J. R., & Miller, P. H. (2010). A developmental perspective on executive function. *Child Development, 81*, 1641–1660.

Carlson, S. M., & Moses, L. J. (2001). Individual differences in inhibitory control and children's theory of mind. *Child Development, 72*, 1032–1053.

Carlson, S. M., Moses, L. J., & Breton, C. (2002). How specific is the relation between executive function and theory of mind?: contributions of inhibitory control and working memory. *Infant and Child Development, 11*, 73–92.

Dunn, J., & Brown, J. (1993). Early conversations about causality: content, pragmatics, and developmental change. *British Journal of Developmental Psychology, 11*, 107–123.

Flavell, J. H. (1981). Cognitive monitoring. In W. P. Dickson (Ed.), *Children's oral communication skills* (pp. 35–60). New York: Academic.

Fodor, J. A. (1983). *The modularity of mind*. Cambridge: MIT Press.

Foley, M., Ratner, H. H., & House, A. T. (2002). Anticipation and source-monitoring errors: children's memory for collaborative activities. *Journal of Cognition and Development, 3*, 385–414.

Ghatala, E. S., Levin, J. R., Pressley, M., & Goodwin, D. (1986). A componential analysis of the effects of derived and supplied strategy-utility information on children's strategy selections. *Journal of Experimental Child Psychology, 41*, 76–92.

Hughes, C., & Dunn, J. (1997). "Pretend you didn't know": preschoolers' talk about mental states in pretend play. *Cognitive Development, 12*, 477–499.

Humphrey, N. (1983). *Consciousness regained: Chapters in the development of mind*. Oxford: Oxford University Press.

Humphrey, N. (1986). *The inner eye*. London: Faber and Faber.

Koriat, A. (1998). Illusions of knowing: The link between knowledge and metaknowledge. In V. Y. Yzerbyt, G. Lories, & B. Dardenne (Eds.), *Metacognition: Cognitive and social dimensions* (pp. 16–34). London: Sage Publications.

Leslie, A. M. (1994). ToMM, ToBy, and agency: Core architecture and domain specficity. In L. A. Hirschfeld & S. A. Gelman (Eds.), *Mapping the mind: Domain specificity in cognition and culture* (pp. 119–148). New York: Cambridge University Press.

Lillard, A. (1999). Developing a cultural theory of mind: the CIAO approach. *Current Directions in Psychological Science, 8*, 57–61.

Mandler, G. (2002). *Consciousness recovered: Psychological functions and origins of conscious thought*. Amsterdam: John Benjamins Publishing Company.

McGivern, J. E., Levin, J. R., Pressley, M., & Ghatala, E. S. (1990). A developmental study of memory monitoring and strategy selection. *Contemporary Educational Psychology, 15*, 103–115.

Moore, C. (2006). *The development of commonsense psychology*. Mahwah: Lawrence Erlbaum Associates.

Nelson, T. O., Kruglanski, A. W., & Jost, J. T. (1998). Knowing thyself and others: Progress in metacognitive social psychology. In V. Y. Yzerbyt, G. Lories, & D. Benoit (Eds.), *Metacognition: Cognitive and social dimensions* (pp. 69–89). London: Sage Publications.

Palincsar, A. S., & Magnusson, S. J. (2001). The interplay of first-hand and second-hand investigations to model and support the development of scientific knowledge and reasoning. In S. M. Carver & D. Klahr (Eds.), *Cognition and instruction: Twenty-five years of progress*. Mahwah: Erlbaum.

Perner, J. (1991). *Understanding the representational mind*. Cambridge: The MIT Press.

Pillow, B. H., & Anderson, K. L. (2006). Children's awareness of their own certainty and understanding of deduction and guessing. *British Journal of Developmental Psychology, 24,* 823–849.

Pressley, M., Ross, K. A., Levin, J. R., & Ghatala, E. S. (1984). The role of strategy-utility knowledge in children's decision making. *Journal of Experimental Child Psychology, 38,* 491–504.

Ratner, H. H., Foley, M. A., & Gimpert, N. (2002). The role of collaborative planning in children's source monitoring errors and learning. *Journal of Experimental Child Psychology, 81,* 44–73.

Rogoff, B. (1990). *Apprenticeship in thinking: Cognitive development in social context*. New York: Oxford University Press.

Saffran, J. R. (2003). Statistical learning: mechanisms and constraints. *Current Directions in Psychological Science, 12,* 110–114.

Salonen, P., Vauras, M., & Efklides, A. (2005). Social interaction: what can it tell us about metacognition and coregulation in learning? *European Psychologist, 10,* 199–208.

Schwanenflugel, P. J., Fabricius, W. V., & Noyes, C. R. (1996). Developing organization of mental verbs: evidence for the development of a constructivist theory of mind in middle childhood. *Cognitive Development, 11,* 265–294.

Tomasello, M. (1999). *The cultural origins of human cognition*. Cambridge: Harvard University Press.

Chapter 6
Conclusion

Abstract In this concluding chapter, three views perspectives on social cognition and development are compared with each other and discussed in relation to the proposed model of interaction among phenomenological awareness, social experience, and conceptual knowledge. These three views are the theory metaphor which describes social understanding as a naïve theory, a perceptual metaphor that view social understanding as based on introspective access, and socio-cultural theories of development that emphasis socially shared knowledge as central to developmental progress. The insights these views provide are amenable to integration. Finally, directions for future research are suggested.

A growing body of research investigates the development of children's understanding of cognitive activities during middle and late childhood. By extending research beyond children's early understanding of mental states, this work has the potential to link studies of young children's social cognitive development with investigations of elementary school children's metacognitive abilities and adolescents' and adults' epistemological thought. As with other areas of children's knowledge, three fundamental questions about development are: (a) what changes occur in children's understanding?, (b) what information do children utilize for learning?, and (c) what learning processes underlie conceptual change? I begin this concluding chapter by briefly summarizing my views on these questions, as they pertain to children's understanding of cognitive activities. Then I consider three general approaches to conceptualizing children's knowledge about the mind: (a) a theory metaphor, (b) a perceptual metaphor, and (c) socio-cultural theories. Finally, I identify issues for future research.

B. H. Pillow, *Children's Discovery of the Active Mind,*
SpringerBriefs in Child Development, DOI: 10.1007/978-1-4614-2248-8_6,
© Bradford H. Pillow 2012

6.1 Developmental Questions

First, to address the question of what changes occur during development, I have distinguished among knowledge of the occurrence of cognitive activities, knowledge of the organization of cognitive activities, and epistemological thought. Although these three levels of understanding are not intended as discrete stages, they do suggest a trend toward increasingly integrated and abstract knowledge. There may be many changes within each level as well. For example, within occurrence knowledge, understanding of particular cognitive activities, such as attention, memory, the stream of consciousness, inference, etc., may develop along somewhat different trajectories. As children develop organizational knowledge, different dimensions of comparison, such as information processing or certainty, may emerge or take on greater emphasis at different times (Schwanenflugel et al. 1998). Epistemological development may include both general patterns of thought across content domains and domain-specific changes in reasoning and conceptions of knowledge (e.g., Hofer 2000; Schommer and Walker 1995). Second, regarding the question of what information children draw upon to learn about cognitive activities, I have proposed that both children's first-person experience of their own mental life and children's social experience provide information that contributes to learning. Moreover, first-person phenomenological awareness and social experience gain enhanced meaning when combined with each other and with children's existing conceptual knowledge. To understand the developmental progression from mental state reasoning to knowledge of cognitive activities and epistemological reflection, the growth of children's knowledge of cognitive functioning needs to be integrated with the development of cognitive monitoring and related to processes of social influence. Moreover, each of these three components is multifaceted and can participate in many patterns of influence during development. Consequently, there is not a single causal pathway. Instead, advances in metacognitive and social cognitive functioning emerge through the accumulation of a variety of experiences involving several possible patterns of influence. Third, with respect to mechanisms of development, I have suggested that general pattern detection processes in conjunction with executive function may enable children to construct concepts of cognitive activities from the available input.

6.2 Three Perspectives on Children's Understanding of the Mind

There remains another general conceptual issue, however; how should the form of children's knowledge about cognitive activities, and the mind more generally, be characterized? While empirical research on children's understanding of cognition of the sort reviewed in Chap. 3 primarily aims to describe the content of children's metacognitive knowledge, developmental theories have characterized such knowledge variously as taking the form of a naive theory, simulation of other minds, or a collaborative social construction. In the present framework, I attempt to combine insights from these three approaches to conceptualizing social cognitive development. First, a theory metaphor has been commonly used to characterize children's understanding of the mind. According to the theory metaphor, knowledge of the mind takes the form of an intuitive theory (e.g., Gopnik 1993; Perner 1991; Wellman 1990). People possess a conceptual understanding of the mind that includes concepts of mental states and concepts of cognitive activities. This understanding is organized around causal connections among mental states, cognitive activities, and actions. Developmental change involves the elaboration of children's existing theory or the construction of new theories. Thus, the theory metaphor emphasizes the content, organization, and transformation of conceptual knowledge. Second, according to a perceptual metaphor, knowledge of the mind takes the form of self-perception, or first-person awareness of one's own mental functioning (e.g., Harris 1991; Humphrey 1983, 1986; Johnson 1988). Phenomenological awareness is seen as a coherent source of information that helps to structure knowledge of mental functioning (e.g., Barsalou 1999; Harris 1991; Humphrey 1983, 1986; Johnson 1988). Thus, conscious experience of one's own mind can be used to simulate other persons' experience. This approach emphasizes the role of phenomenological awareness in children's understanding of self and other. Third, socio-cultural theories emphasize intersubjectivity and the appropriation of cultural knowledge (e.g., Rogoff 1990; Tomasello 1999b). By achieving a shared perspective with social partners, children can participate in cultural activities and learn cultural beliefs and values. In particular, recognizing a social partner's attitude toward the child's own mental state facilitates communication and learning about mental functioning (e.g., Tomasello 1999a).

As others have noted, these approaches are amenable to integration (e.g., Kuhn 2000; Lillard 1999). The theory metaphor characterizes children as actively constructing their understanding of mental functioning from available evidence. Therefore, identifying the experiences that inform the growth of children's conceptual knowledge is an important issue for this approach. The theory metaphor is amenable to inclusion of both phenomenological awareness and social experience within the database that informs children's theorizing, and the theory metaphor also highlights the central role of conceptual knowledge in interpreting experience. Because a child's existing theory, or conceptual knowledge, guides attention to and interpretation of particular aspects of experience, conceptual knowledge influences the detection and assimilation of both phenomenological and social cues. The resulting understanding of cognitive functioning is an indirect construction based on mental and social events, rather than a direct reflection of them. Moreover, theories can be communicated through discussion, instruction, and metaphors, and the content of theories may vary across cultures. Thus, the theory metaphor allows for social transmission and cultural variation in the development of children's understanding of cognitive activities.

The perceptual metaphor has the advantage of positing a non-arbitrary relationship between knowledge of mental processes and first-person experience of mental life. This correspondence occurs in two ways. First, children's own conscious experience is taken to be a fundamental form of social understanding. For example, Johnson (1988) argues that intuitive knowledge of the mind derives from conscious access to the structure of subjective experience. Barsalou (1999) suggests that during introspection selective attention may be attracted to innately constrained dimensions of experience, including both representational states and cognitive operations. Second, because adults' understanding of mental functioning also is rooted in first-person experience, socially transmitted beliefs about cognition would bear a non-arbitrary relation to adults' phenomenological experience. Therefore, basing knowledge, at least partly, on phenomenological awareness would facilitate social transmission of beliefs about cognitive functioning. Both children's and adult's metacognitive knowledge would be similarly structured, though at different levels of sophistication. When adults express beliefs about cognitive activities to children, children's own first person experience would ground their comprehension of adults' mentalistic references. In addition, the perceptual metaphor allows for developmental improvements in cognitive monitoring. On this metaphor, improvements in knowledge would involve a process akin to perceptual learning. Over time children might notice and conceptualize more features of conscious experience. Because phenomenological awareness of cognitive activities is limited and indirect, interpretation of metacognitive experiences is influenced by conceptual knowledge of mental functioning and by social experiences.

With their emphasis on intersubjectivity, socio-cultural theories complement the theory and perceptual metaphors. Rather than being solely individually created, insights into the mind also may be collaboratively constructed and shared across individuals. The experience of intersubjectivity facilitates social interaction and also informs the development of individual knowledge about mental functioning. Placing children's understanding of cognition in a social and cultural context is critical for explaining how children make analogies between self and other, as suggested by Lillard (1999), Meltzoff and Moore (1997), Moore (2006), and Tomasello (1999a), and how children learn cultural beliefs about the mind. At the same time, as Astington and Olson (1995), Kuhn (2000), Barresi and Moore (1996) have observed, an adequate account of socially constructed meaning must integrate the concepts and cognitive activities of individual participants as part of the collaborative process. Thus, consideration of children's individual conceptual understanding of cognitive functioning and monitoring of phenomenological awareness enhances efforts to understand social influences on development.

6.3 Directions for Future Research

By relating children's conceptual knowledge of cognitive activities to children's phenomenological awareness and social experience, the present framework suggests several issues for future research. Developmental changes in each component of the framework need to be described in detail from early childhood through adolescence, and relations among the components need to be investigated. Although a body of research on children's conceptual understanding of cognitive activities is growing, children's understanding of different activities typically is investigated in separate studies. Systematic examination of patterns of change throughout the course of childhood remains to be done. Research examining temporal and functional relations among children's concepts of several different cognitive activities, such as attention, memory, inference, and the stream of consciousness, etc., would provide a more complete and coherent picture of developmental patterns. Children's knowledge of a wider range of cognitive activities, including planning, reading comprehension, mathematical problem solving, and cognitive monitoring, is worthy of investigation. Furthermore, making clear distinctions among occurrence, organizational, and epistemological knowledge, and also identifying specific facets of each of these three forms of knowledge, will facilitate efforts to trace patterns of developmental change. In addition to examining age-related changes in occurrence, organizational, and epistemological knowledge, it is also important to investigate developmental relations among these forms of knowledge. To determine if and how the development of one form of conceptual knowledge influences the development of the other forms, particular attention should be paid to developmental transitions. Training, longitudinal, and microgenetic studies may be useful for this purpose. Because each of these three forms of knowledge is multifaceted, transitions are likely to be gradual and complex.

Children's source monitoring, comprehension monitoring, and memory monitoring have been studied extensively; however, certainty monitoring and effort and difficulty monitoring have been studied relatively little. Moreover, the literature often appears fragmented, with different aspects of monitoring being studied at different ages. Comprehensive studies over broad age ranges are needed. Also, implicit measures of monitoring (e.g., non-verbal behaviors such as facial expression or hesitation) and explicit judgments should be assessed in the same study and related to each other and to children's conceptual knowledge. Information about age-related changes in what aspects of cognitive functioning children monitor effectively would provide a foundation for detailed studies of what children learn about cognitive activities through monitoring. Relations between specific aspects of monitoring and specific aspects of metacognitive knowledge need to be examined. For example, certainty monitoring might be related to (a) children's knowledge about the certainty of specific cognitive activities, such as deduction or guessing, (b) the extent to which children organize their knowledge of cognitive activities along a certainty dimension, or (c) adolescents' tendency to reflect on the general possibility of certain knowledge. Source monitoring might be important for learning about the occurrence and typical effects of specific cognitive activities, or to the tendency to organize metacognitive knowledge along an input–output dimension. The bidirectional relationship between monitoring and metacognitive knowledge also should be investigated over time to determine how knowledge acquisition influences children's phenomenological awareness of cognitive activity.

The social and cultural context of metacognitive development deserves extensive study. Existing research on mentalistic references during early childhood conversations provides a starting point for tracing developmental changes in the content and structure of psychological discussions throughout childhood. Descriptive information about how and in what contexts adults and children refer to cognitive activities during naturally occurring conversations would lay the groundwork for correlational studies examining developmental relations between conversational variables and the growth of metacognitive knowledge. Natural language studies should examine the context and structure of mentalistic talk, as well as the frequency of usage for mental terms. Discourse in both academic and non-academic settings should be considered, and language studies should be complemented by efforts to identify patterns of non-verbal behavior that might provide cues to changes in an actor's mental state. Such cues might suggest the occurrence of cognitive activities mediating changes in mental state. Cultural variations in the nature and use of psychological references during conversation, and the socialization of social understanding more generally, also remain to be investigated.

Children's practical use of knowledge about cognition in their everyday lives is an important avenue for investigation. Learning about cognitive activities may be useful in both academic and social situations. Socially, reasoning about cognitive processes may aid children in understanding other peoples' behavior, anticipating others' response to the child's own behavior, or explaining children's own thoughts, emotions, and actions to others. Young children's understanding of mental states such as belief and desire has been found to be related to individual differences in social competence and social behavior (e.g., Dunn et al. 1991; Capage and Watson 2001; Cutting and Dunn 1999; Jenkins and Astington 2000; Lalonde and Chandler 1995; Walker 2005; Watson et al. 1999). Furthermore, during late childhood, advanced social understanding is related to social competence (Bosacki and Astington 1999). Academically, knowledge of cognitive processes might help children to comprehend teachers' metacognitive comments, understand scientific reasoning, study effectively, detect and remedy comprehension difficulty, and critically evaluate the arguments and reasoning of both self and others. Metacognitive abilities generally are related to academic performance (e.g., Hacker et al. 2009), and some specific aspects of metacognitive knowledge are related to intellectual ability. For example, high school students' beliefs about learning are related to performance in school; those who appreciate that learning does happen quickly tend to achieve higher grades (Schommer 1993). Several studies indicate that compared to average children elementary school students, intellectually gifted students have greater declarative metacognitive knowledge concerning memory and attention; however, gifted and average children do not appear to differ in the organization of their knowledge of cognitive activities (Alexander et al. 1995). In addition to studies documenting general links between metacognitive knowledge and social adjustment, intellectual ability, or academic performance, studies that investigate relations between children's knowledge of cognition and specific social or academic skill would be valuable. Developmental relations between children's knowledge of cognitive activities and children's social or academic abilities are likely to be subtle and complex. Longitudinal studies should examine relations between age-related in knowledge of cognition and age-related changes in social attributes or academic abilities and relations between individual differences in these characteristics.

Increases in children's conceptual knowledge of cognitive activities, children's monitoring abilities, or children's social skills each may result in new experiences that influence the other two areas of functioning. As a result, patterns of influence among phenomenological awareness, conceptual understanding, and social experience may change with age. Specifying possible patterns of influence in detail should facilitate empirical investigation of precise developmental changes in (a) the particular patterns of influence that occur among phenomenological awareness, conceptual understanding, and social experience, (b) the frequency of particular patterns of influence, and (c) children's ability to learn about cognitive activities from specific combinations of conceptual, phenomenological, and social information. The emphasis here has been on describing age-related changes in knowledge and identifying potential sources of information about cognitive activities. In addition, theorizing about metacognitive development needs to specify the cognitive mechanisms by which different sources of information are integrated and new insights into mental functioning are constructed. Pattern recognition abilities and executive function may facilitate learning about cognitive activities. In addition, processes of theory revision, introspection, and intersubjectivity have been proposed as possible mechanisms of social cognitive development (e.g., Gopnik and Wellman 1992; Harris 1991; Humphrey 1986; Lillard 1999; Tomasello 1999a). These mechanisms need to be articulated more fully and eventually integrated with each other. Detailed empirical evidence about children's use of the patterns of information described in the proposed framework could inform such theoretical efforts.

Finally, to put my thoughts in perspective, I will end with one last comment on mental activity from my son. At 5 years and 8 months of age, Matthew questioned my grasp on reality (unjustly, at least on this particular occasion):

Me: Is that mommy?

Matthew: What?

Me: I thought I heard something in garage. I think mommy's home.

Matthew: I didn't hear anything. Maybe your brain just made it up. It does that sometimes.

References

Alexander, J. M., Carr, M., & Schwanenflugel, P. J. (1995). Development of metacognition in gifted children: directions for future research. *Developmental Review, 15*, 1–37.

Astington, J. W., & Olson, D. R. (1995). The cognitive revolution in children's understanding of the mind. *Human Development, 38*, 179–189.

Barresi, J., & Moore, C. (1996). Intentional relations and social understanding. *Behavioral and Brain Sciences, 19,* 107–154.

Barsalou, L. W. (1999). Perceptual symbol systems. *Behavioral and Brain Sciences, 22,* 577–609.

Bosacki, S., & Astington, J. W. (1999). Theory of mind in preadolescence: relations between social understanding and social competence. *Social Development, 8,* 237–255.

Capage, L., & Watson, A. C. (2001). Individual differences in theory of mind, aggressive behavior, and social skills in young children. *Early Education and Development, 12,* 613–628.

Cutting, A. L., & Dunn, J. (1999). Theory of mind, emotion understanding, language, and family background: individual differences and interrelations. *Child Development, 70,* 853–865.

Dunn, J., Brown, J., Slomkowski, C., Tesla, C., & Youngblade, L. (1991). Young children's understanding of other people's feelings and beliefs: individual differences and their antecedents. *Child Development, 62,* 1352–1366.

Gopnik, A. (1993). How we know our minds: the illusion of first-person knowledge of intentionality. *Behavioral and Brain Sciences, 16,* 1–14.

Gopnik, A., & Wellman, H. M. (1992). Why the child's theory of mind really is a theory. *Mind and Language, 7,* 145–171.

Hacker, D. J., Dunlosky, J., & Graesser, A. C. (2009). *Handbook of metacognition in education.* New York: Taylor and Francis Group.

Harris, P. (1991). The work of the imagination. In A. Whiten (Ed.), *Natural theories of mind: Evolution, development, and simulation of everyday mindreading* (pp. 283–304). Cambridge: Basil Blackwell.

Hofer, B. K. (2000). Dimensionality and disciplinary differences in personal epistemology. *Contemporary Educational Psychology, 25,* 378–405.

Humphrey, N. (1983). *Consciousness regained: Chapters in the development of mind.* Oxford: Oxford University Press.

Humphrey, N. (1986). *The inner eye.* London: Faber and Faber.

Jenkins, J. M., & Astington, J. W. (2000). Theory of mind and social behavior: causal models tested in a longitudinal study. *Merrill-Palmer Quarterly, 46,* 203–220.

Johnson, C. N. (1988). Theory of mind and the structure of conscious experience. In J. W. Astington, P. L. Harris, & D. R. Olson (Eds.), *Developing theories of mind* (pp. 47–63). New York: Cambridge University Press.

Kuhn, D. (2000). Theory of mind, metacognition, and reasoning: A life-span perspective. In P. Mitchell & K. J. Riggs (Eds.), *Children's reasoning and the mind* (pp. 301–326). Hove: Psychology Press.

Lalonde, C. E., & Chandler, M. J. (1995). False belief understanding goes to school: on the socio-emotional consequences of coming early or late to a first theory of mind. *Cognition and Emotion, 9,* 167–185.

Lillard, A. (1999). Developing a cultural theory of mind: the CIAO approach. *Current Directions in Psychological Science, 8,* 57–61.

Meltzoff, A. N., & Moore, M. K. (1997). Explaining facial imitation: a theoretical model. *Early Development and Parenting, 6,* 179–192.

Moore, C. (2006). *The development of commonsense psychology.* Mahwah: Lawrence.

Perner, J. (1991). *Understanding the representational mind.* Cambridge: The MIT Press.

Rogoff, B. (1990). *Apprenticeship in thinking: Cognitive development in social context.* New York: Oxford University Press.

Schommer, M. (1993). Epistemological development and academic performance among secondary students. *Journal of Educational Psychology, 85,* 406–411.

Schommer, M., & Walker, K. (1995). Are epistemological beliefs similar across domains? *Journal of Educational Psychology, 87,* 424–432.

Schwanenfugel, P. J., Henderson, R. L., & Fabricius, W. V. (1998). Developing organization of mental verbs and theory of mind in middle childhood: evidence from extensions. *Developmental Psychology, 34,* 512–524.

Tomasello, M. (1999a). Having intentions, understanding intentions, and understanding communicative intentions. In P. D. Zelazo, J. W. Astington, & D. R. Olson (Eds.),

Developing theories of intention: Social understanding and self-control (pp. 63–76). Mahwah: Lawrence Erlbaum Associates.

Tomasello, M. (1999b). *The cultural origins of human cognition*. Cambridge: Harvard University Press.

Walker, S. (2005). Gender differences in the relationship between young children's peer-related social competence and individual differences in theory of mind. *The Journal of Genetic Psychology, 166*, 297–312.

Watson, A. C., Nixon, C. L., Wilson, A., & Capage, L. (1999). Social interaction skills and theory of mind in young children. *Developmental Psychology, 35*, 386–391.

Wellman, H. M. (1990). *The child's theory of mind*. Cambridge: MIT Press.